Anxiety In Relationship

Learn How to Identify, overcome and eliminate Jealousy, Negative thinking and Couple conflicts.

Rebecca Hudson

© **Copyright 2020 by Rebecca Hudson - All rights reserved.**

The content contained within this book may not be reproduced, duplicated, or transmitted without direct written permission from the author or the publisher.

Under no circumstances will any blame or legal responsibility be held against the publisher, or author, for any damages, reparation, or monetary loss due to the information contained within this book. Either directly or indirectly. You are responsible for your own choices, actions, and results.

Legal Notice:

This book is copyright protected. This book is only for personal use. You cannot amend, distribute, sell, use, quote or paraphrase any part, or the content within this book, without the consent of the author or publisher.

Disclaimer Notice:

Please note the information contained within this document is for educational and entertainment purposes only. All effort has been executed to present accurate, up to date, and reliable, complete information. No warranties of any kind are declared or implied.

Readers acknowledge that the author is not engaging in the endearing of legal, financial, medical, or professional advice. The content within this book has been derived from various sources.

Please consult a licensed professional before attempting any techniques outlined in this book.

By reading this document, the reader agrees that under no circumstances is the author responsible for any losses, direct or indirect, which are incurred as a result of the use of the information contained within this document, including, but not limited to, — errors, omissions, or inaccuracies.

Table of Contents

Introduction..9

Chapter 1..12

- **Why Anxiety Starts in a Relationship**
  - How Anxiety Starts in a Relationship
  - 1.2 An Insecure Partner
  - 1.3 Attachment
  - 1.4 Happiness in Love
  - 1.5 Love Dismissing
  - 1.6 No Need for Love Fearful
  - 1.7 Conflicted in Love
  - 1.8 Styles of Attachment

Chapter 2: 42

- **Why Anxiety Can Take Over Your Relationship**
  - 2.1 A Supportive Partner

Chapter 3: 52

- **How to change yourself to reduce the toxicity in your relationship**
  - 3.1 See Yourself in a different way
  - 3.2 Do You really Know Yourself?
  - 3.3 Observe Yourself

- 3.4 The Most Common Problem in a Relationship
- 3.5 Be Aware of Your Patterns

Chapter 4: 75

❖ **<u>Overcome Obstacles in Your Relationship</u>**
- 4.1 Discover Hidden Problems In A Relationship
- 4.2 How Pain Can Change People
- 4.3 Be Open to New Experiences
- 4.4 Tips to Overcome Problems in a Relationship
- 4.5 Listen
- 4.6 Avoid the blame game Spend time together
- 4.7 Make sure you're on the same page
- 4.8 Enjoy

Chapter 5: 95

❖ **<u>Create a Sense of Security for Your Relationship</u>**
- 5.1 Self-Awareness
- 5.2 Thoughts and Emotions, which differences?
- 5.3 Control your feelings
- 5.3 Identify your feelings
- 5.4 self-Compassion
- 5.5 Practice mindfulness

- 5.6 Self-Compassion and his Power

Chapter 6: 117

❖ **Develop Self-Awareness**
- 6.1 Vulnerability
- 6.2 Your Feelings
- 6.3 Prepare yourself to endure and persevere through difficult emotions.
- 6.3 Use Your Thoughts to make friends
- 6.4 Change Your Thoughts immediately

Chapter 7: 132

❖ **Communication is the key for an Happy Relationship**
- 7.1 Self-Disclosure
- 7.2 Rewards of Self-Disclosure Listening Skills
- 7.3 Pseudo-Listening vs. Real Listening
- 7.4 Listening Blocks
- 7.5 Active Listening
- 7.6 Paraphrasing
- 7.7 Clarifying
- 7.8 Feedback
- 7.9 Expressing Your Needs Validation
- 7.10 Empathy Apologize

Chapter 8: 149

❖ **Why Cultivate the Self-Compassion its so important**
- 8.1 Why you have to practice Generosity
- 8.2 Kindness Self-Care to treat yourself
- 8.3 Why you have to introduce Self-Care in to Your Life
- 8.4 Stay Strong
- 8.5 Feed Your Spirit
- 8.6 The importance of gratitude

Chapter 9: 167

❖ **Light Up Your Love Life**
- 9.1 Relationship Goals
- 9.2 The perfect Romantic Partner
- 9.3 Perfect Relationship
- 9.4 How to Find Support

Chapter 10: 180

❖ **Keep Your Relationship alive**
- 10.1 Discover Yourself Relying on Each Other
- 10.2 Boost your Intimacy
- 10.3 You have to find Your Anxious Attachment
- 10.4 Self-Reliance

- 10.5 Close Connection
- 10.6 Keep yourself engaged
- 10.7 Share experiences with your partner
- 10.8 Why you have to Work on a project with your partner
- 10.9 make visible actions for love
- 10.10 Express always your feelings of love and happiness
- 10.11 Compliment your partner
- 10.12 Find new ways to show all your love
- 10.12 Know when to yield

Chapter 11: 192

❖ **<u>Why you have to resolve the differences between you and your partner</u>**
- 11.1 Support
- 11.2 Show Empathy
- 11.3 Forgive
- 11.4 How to Know If Your Relationship Is Really Worth It
- 11.5 Ending Note
- 11.6 Talk with a Professional

Conclusion..202

Introduction

Chances are, you've been romantically involved with someone at some point in your life. Hence, it's likely that you're well-versed in the anxiety and paranoia that accompanies such a relationship. Not all relationships are the same, but it's safe to say that most of them are filled with turmoil and hardships. Throughout the research process for this book, we had the chance to study hundreds of relationships, and one thing became apparent. The number one factor that sucks the happiness out of any relationship is anxiety.

My Book "Anxiety in Relationships" focuses on identifying the factors that determine your attachment style and recognizing the issues that cause anxiety in your relationship.

From the beginning of time, humans have paired up for crucial acts such as perpetuating the species and the division of labor to stay alive and safe.

Over time, this type of relationship has suffered many hardships and faced many trials. With this book, we want to help you solve the most common issues faced by twenty-first-century couples.

Learn How to Feel Secure by Uncovering the Blocks Preventing You From a Loving Union.

Even the most emotionally mature people can sometimes feel insecure or a lack of stability in their relationship. When anxiety strikes, you may start to wonder what's wrong with you and why your relationships don't last long.

It is also not uncommon for people to have been in a relationship for a long time but still feel a void inside them. Both single and committed people are prone to thinking that they will never be happy in a relationship.

Everyone wants a successful relationship—one that is stable, committed, and honest. People want a partner to share their lives with, and experience all the adventures life has to offer with them.

At the same time though, people hesitate to show their real selves to their partners, to let themselves be vulnerable, and they worry that their demons might destroy the relationship.

That's where we come in. We will help you tackle the problems in your relationship, manage your anxiety, and the stress that comes with it. If you're looking for comfort, reassurance, and support but don't know where to start, this book is for you.

We have compiled this book in a way that resonates with anyone who is unhappy or unsatisfied in their relationship.

This book is a great tool that can help you change your mindset, rediscover the spark in your relationship, and heal from within. It will also help you make wise choices when choosing your partner, one who will offer you genuine love, affection, and support as you grow together.

This book contains our proven formula for finding the right partner, understanding them, and making changes in yourself to ensure a stable relationship. This formula has consistently proven more fruitful than all those articles you see on the Internet.

The way we usually learn about relationships is through first-hand experience.

Since we develop relationships all through our lives, this is a constant, continuous process. The first relationship that you developed was likely with your parents or primary caregivers.

This is when you probably learned about the warmth, love, and insecurities of a relationship. The process continued into your teenage years and then on to your adult life. We want to help you understand the different types of relationships so you can have a pleasant experience with your romantic partner.

This book is not only geared towards people who are looking for a stable relationship, though. It will also teach you practical communication skills, help you navigate the struggles of a relationship, and overcome your fear of rejection.

Chapter 1: Why Anxiety Starts in a Relationship

Anxiety is your mind and body's natural reaction to stressful or dangerous situations. It is a normal response that we all experience at one time or another throughout our lives. However, when an anxiety disorder exists, it can take a heavy toll, both mentally and physically.

Anxiety disorders are characterized by excessive fear of real or imagined events that can cause minor or drastic changes in a person's life.

One of the most common symptoms is what's known as an anxiety attack, which a person can experience even when they aren't facing any immediate danger. When something triggers an anxiety attack, the person will usually experience feelings of panic, accompanied by physical symptoms such as sweaty palms, trembling, nausea, elevated heart rate, pain, and difficulty breathing.

Anxiety attacks aren't permanent and usually last anywhere from a few minutes to a

few hours.

People of all ages can suffer from anxiety disorders, and there are many different causes and triggers for them. For example, the most common reasons for anxiety in children and teens are the pressure to do well in school, bullying from classmates or teachers, sibling rivalry, and upcoming exams. Many young children also face separation anxiety, which happens when the child gets permanently or temporarily separated from one or both parents.

For adults, the causes of anxiety disorders tend to be work-related. Other common reasons for anxiety include traumatic events, the need to meet expectations or fear of failure.

These situations exert immense pressure on the person's psyche, and their fear levels rise as a result. Their mental health suffers and they begin to do poorly in school or work.

In addition to psychological damage, their physical health will take a hit as well. Stomach problems, erratic heart rate, shortness of breath, nausea, sleeping disorders, and fatigue are all physical manifestations of an anxiety disorder.

There are plenty of things you can do if you or the people close to you display symptoms of an anxiety disorder. Psychotherapy is the best course of action if you see signs of depression or anxiety in yourself or your loved ones. Depending on the severity of the symptoms, a psychiatrist might also prescribe medication.

Anti-anxiety medication can provide quick and effective relief from panic attacks, as well as long-term stability. Your psychiatrist will manage the dosage of these treatments and make adjustments as you progress.

We can further classify anxiety disorders into the following types:

• Generalized Anxiety Disorder (GAD) is a type of anxiety disorder in which a person endures a constant state of stress and depression without any apparent problems or stressors.

People suffering from generalized anxiety disorder find it difficult to sleep and relax their minds. Common symptoms of GAD include shortness of breath, headaches, muscle pain, nausea, trembling, sweating, irritability, and lightheadedness.

• Panic Disorder (PD) is a severe type of anxiety disorder that causes excessive and unexpected terror, which keeps the individual

in a state of near-constant fear. This type of anxiety disorder makes the individual unable to make any life decisions. A person with Panic Disorder usually avoids specific situations that can trigger a panic attack.

Significant symptoms of panic disorder include sweating, trembling, shortness of breath, lightheadedness, GAD, headaches, muscle pain, chest pain, and increased heart rate. People who have Panic Disorder can have a significant fear of sudden death or losing their mental health. Drug abuse, depression, and alcoholism are common problems among people living with PD.

• Agoraphobia is a type of anxiety disorder in which the individual restricts themselves from performing daily activities to the point where they stay indoors for weeks or even months. In this way, they believe they can avoid any situations that can trigger a panic attack.

• Social Anxiety is a type of anxiety disorder which mostly triggers in social events and gatherings. It stems from the fear of being humiliated or rejected by other people. This makes the individual stay away from parties, dinners, or any social gatherings where the person feels that they will be scrutinized. It is important to note that Social Anxiety is not the same thing as shyness.

Social Anxiety can adversely affect the individual's relationships with their loved ones. It drives a wedge between them and those who love them and want to help them overcome this disorder.

That's why it's vital to discuss anxiety symptoms with loved ones. Timely and effective treatment is crucial for people with Social Anxiety to recover their relationships and social life.

• Obsessive-Compulsive Disorder (OCD) is a condition in which the individual becomes unable to control their behavior and actions.

Individuals suffering from OCD unintentionally develop certain habits that become part of their routine. Some habits include washing their

hands over and over, repeatedly checking or verifying that things are a certain way, and continuously experiencing negative or obtrusive thoughts.

• Post-Traumatic Stress Disorder (PTSD) is caused by a traumatic event in a person's life. A particular memory or flashback associated with the event can trigger a panic attack. People with PTSD display heightened irritability and emotional or physical outbursts when undergoing a panic attack. Drug abuse and depression are common problems of people living with PTSD.

All the above types of anxiety are listed based on their intensity.

Anxiety varies from mild to severe and has different effects on each person. As mentioned before, anxiety is an entirely natural behavior that all human beings experience and is sometimes necessary to help identify potential danger.

It only becomes dangerous and harmful when it crosses a limit and becomes symptomatic. If you believe that you are experiencing symptoms of anxiety, we recommend that you seek professional help.

1.1 How Anxiety Starts in a Relationship

Nobody wants to lose their connections with family, friends, and loved ones. Still, the sad thing is that this sometimes happens without us knowing the reasons why. There will always be ups and downs, rude or unkind behaviors, financial problems, work or school pressures, and many other problems in any relationship. We all have different life experiences and go through different mental states throughout the day.

Some of these experiences are painful or even traumatic. They can lead to emotional outbursts or unhealthy behaviors that can drive the people around us away. When these behaviors become a regular part of your interactions with your loved ones, they can begin to have a potentially permanent effect on your relationships.

Suppose your partner has never experienced a mental illness. In that case, it can be difficult for them to understand what you're going through.

For example, depression and anxiety often make the person withdraw from social life and their loved ones, which might be very difficult for their significant other to comprehend.

Obsessive thoughts and tendencies are also symptoms of anxiety disorders. It's human nature to want to give and receive love and affection.

However, some people can become overly possessive over people and things, which leads to feelings of jealousy and insecurity. When they aren't getting the desired love and attention from their loved ones, they start feeling anxious. They can also experience anxiety or panic attacks when they think they're being avoided or neglected. This is one of the most common causes of anxiety in relationships.

Excessive attachment to a romantic partner is also indicative of an anxiety disorder. Thoughts of separation or not getting the desired attention and responses from their partner can profoundly affect people who suffer from anxiety disorders. A psychotherapist can offer tips to help you be a grounding, supportive presence for your loved one if something triggers an attack.

Asking what they need from you, and providing love, support, and understanding are crucial when helping a loved one through their symptoms of anxiety and fear. However, keep in mind that severe panic attacks should be immediately reported to their treating specialist.

Self-confidence—or lack thereof—is yet another primary reason for anxiety in a relationship. For many people, anxiety comes from low self-esteem and the belief that they aren't "good enough." As such, meeting new people is often an excruciating ordeal.

These feelings of insecurity and inferiority can cause severe stress and depression.

However, you must keep in mind that your low self-esteem is only a product of mental illness. Talk-therapy is a fantastic way to learn to

overcome your feelings of insecurity and learn true self-love and acceptance.

Do you ever fear that you aren't "good enough" for your significant other? Or that they "deserve better"? Try talking to your significant other about how you feel. Overcoming these issues can be easier with the right care, support, and attention from family and friends, in addition to therapy and medication. Never take your mental health

lightly—opening up to the people who love and care about you is the first step to recovery.

A healthy romantic relationship is one that can roll with the punches, handle the ups and downs, and not be destroyed by the inevitable end of the "honeymoon phase."

Many people entering a new relationship talk about that "butterflies in the stomach" feeling when their new love interest so much as walks by. You have probably experienced it yourself. You want this feeling to last forever and for your relationship to be absolutely perfect. You go out of your way to make the best impression, sometimes at the expense of your true feelings. Maybe you start changing some aspects of yourself to fit with your new partner. You begin second-guessing every decision you make.

This level of stress at the beginning of a relationship is not healthy and can lead to even more serious problems later on.

Here are some things you can do to overcome the stress of starting a new relationship.

First, you have to identify the root cause of your anxiety and your fears of not being the right person for your partner.

When you meet someone you like, you will naturally want to develop a relationship

with that person. As you continue with your relationship, you might start thinking negative things about yourself. The bad memories may begin to pop up, reminding you of things you're not proud of, making you feel unworthy of love.

All these negative thoughts are unreliable, though. More often than not, they come from your anxiety disorder or depression.

You have to face them head-on and not let them rule your life—and ruin your relationship.

If there's something in your past that you feel ashamed of, you'll likely experience the fear that your partner will find out about it. While it's important to keep in mind that you are in no way obligated to share every single aspect of your past with your significant other, sometimes keeping a big secret can be very stressful and ultimately harmful to you and your relationship.

The best way to tackle this situation is to share this past event with your partner when you feel safe and ready to do so.

Consider talking to your significant other about any factor in your life that brings your stress before you decide that you're a bad boyfriend or girlfriend.

Talking about a painful or shameful event in your past can take a

massive load off your chest and set your mind at ease. Not only that, but opening up and sharing with your partner can help strengthen your bond.

You know you have found a keeper when your partner goes out of their way to try to understand your mental state and help you cope with the stress. Step by step, as you feel ready to do so, share your feelings and hidden truths about yourself. Ask your partner to go on a walk or dinner and start a discussion in a pleasant and safe setting. When your partner realizes that you're asking for their support, you might just be surprised when they meet you halfway.

However, keep in mind that your partner is likely not a licensed therapist and thus will be unable to provide you with all the help you need. That's where therapists come in.

Identifying and treating the root causes of anxiety disorders can be a lifesaver for both you and your partner's mental and physical health.

In the long run, it will also be very beneficial for your relationship.

Ignoring the symptoms of anxiety disorders in you or your partner can be very damaging to both of you as individuals and as a couple.

Let's say that it's not you, but your partner who is suffering from an anxiety disorder. Chances are they feel alone and unloved if they perceive a lack of support from you. Some people are used to keeping their feelings well under wraps, even from their significant others. Such people are at risk of ultimately damaging their relationship if they keep choosing not to open up to their partners. None of us are mind readers though, and it can be unfair to expect our partners to notice that something is bothering us.

It's always best for us to discuss our condition and worries with our partner to get support. A lack of communication can cause distance and also increase misinterpretations. To maintain a healthy relationship with your partner, you should share your feelings and emotions with them. Relationships that are based on trust and honesty are the ones that stand the test of time.

Another significant side effect of depression and anxiety is the lack of sex drive or disinterest in sex.

The key here is to increase communication with your significant other. Regular sex or romance helps remove a large portion of the stress and anxiety. If you're not in the mood of sex, communicate with your partner and convey your message. It might not always be perfect, but if your partner loves you, they will understand.

1.2 An Insecure Partner

Unlike other ailments, anxiety disorders cannot be tested through blood, X-rays, or any other lab tests. Anxiety is a psychological disorder that can only be diagnosed by identifying its symptoms. Timely and effective treatment can help the individual to manage and even successfully beat this disorder.

Here are some points that can help you identify the symptoms of anxiety disorder in you or your partner.

• Anxiety - Anxiety is your body's response to triggers like fear, stress, depression, and traumatic experiences. When you enter a new relationship, you might notice signs of nervousness in you or your new partner.

Nerves and jitters are completely normal in any budding relationship. Still, there are certain thoughts or behaviors that exceed the norm and begin to tread into anxiety disorder territory.

For instance, you might experience random negative thoughts that this new relationship will never be successful or long-lasting because you "aren't good enough" or "don't deserve a happy relationship."

Eventually, due to a lack of communication or fear of rejection, you

will feel the burden of carrying the entire relationship on your shoulders.

You could even start thinking that you have to change yourself to fit the other person. You will believe that the success of your relationship is solely your responsibility. When you start feeling that way, your relationship will steadily head toward anxiety and stress.

- Lack of self-confidence - Lack of confidence or low self-esteem can drive a wedge between you and your significant other. A lack of self-

confidence affects a person's ability to build a strong relationship with others, especially romantic partners. Because you feel you're not good enough for them, you begin to feel jealous of the people around them, who you think are "better than you."

If you or your partner suffer from low self-esteem, a need for constant reassurance might arise. If you want to keep your relationship from being damaged, you need to be patient with an insecure partner. Try to support and validate them as much as you can to boost up their self-confidence. When you feel the liberty to do so, you can also suggest they seek professional help to get to the bottom of their insecurity issues.

- Poor communication - It's human nature to want to connect to

other people. We are, after all, creatures that thrive on community and connection to one another. So when we find a romantic interest, it's only natural to want to establish a link by communicating our thoughts and feelings with them and having them do the same with us.

However, when one or both parties in a romantic relationship find it difficult to communicate, the relationship will slowly fall apart. If you can't share your thoughts, feelings, personal problems, past traumas, hopes, or dreams with your significant other, a gap will open between you, which can become a reason for a breakup.

Most misunderstandings in relationships come about due to a lack of communication.

Try having healthy, honest, and constant conversations with your partner. This is a crucial first step to solving all kinds of problems and can also help you avoid new misunderstandings.

• Lack of respect - Disrespecting your partner involves any rude or impolite behavior that disregards or hurts their feelings. Respect is the core principle of any healthy and happy relationship. If you find that your partner's words and actions show no regard for your feelings, thoughts, or beliefs, try having a conversation with them. Clearly point out to them what part of their behavior you found disrespectful and ask them not to do it again.

In many cases though, for one reason or another, people fail to draw the line at the early stages of the relationship, when the behavior first takes place. In the worst cases, that initial lack of respect can ultimately lead to physical and psychological abuse.

Likewise, always remember to be respectful of your partner. Don't look down on their feelings just because you don't understand them. Instead, try asking them why they feel the way they do and keep an open heart and mind to what they have to tell you.

• Lack of consent - Entering a new romantic relationship sometimes also means the beginning of a new sexual relationship. However, being in a relationship with someone does not mean you have an automatic pass to sex whenever you want it.

The same goes for your partner. Getting consent is vital for a healthy, happy, and successful sexual relationship.

Be respectful of your partner's boundaries, and demand that yours be respected as well. Don't force each other into something you're not ready for, that makes you uncomfortable, or that you're simply not in the mood for.

We all move at a different pace after all, and honoring each other's wishes is a key ingredient for a nurturing bond.

1.3 Attachment

The way we form attachments to other people varies from person to person. We all have different ways of expressing affection, which leads to varying interpretations of what it means to have a successful relationship. Often, we'll look for a romantic partner who has a compatible attachment style to ours.

This is not always the case, though. Sometimes we'll find ourselves attracted to someone who we consider to be our polar opposite. If we don't keep an open mind and an open line of communication with our significant other, misunderstandings are bound to arise.

This chapter will cover the four different styles of attachments so you can have a deeper understanding of them. After identifying the key characteristics of different relationships, you will be able to identify your own style of attachment, as well as your partner's.

It is vitally important that you are honest with yourself about your attachment style. As we have mentioned before, it isn't uncommon for people to withhold some aspects of themselves, or completely alter themselves to fit better with their partner.

But this artificiality will be a major cause of trouble later on in the relationship.

Keeping up the facade and pretending to be someone you're not, is unsustainable and will take a heavy toll on your mental health.

An ideal approach to reduce the anxiety that you might feel about being "perfect" for your partner is first to understand yourself. After reading and understanding the four basic styles of attachment, you will find your own and eventually find the attachment style you would like in a romantic partner.

While evaluating your style of attachment, take some time to understand the other types as well.

Try to identify your present or past partners' attachment style or even your close family and friends'. Your attachment-related anxiety can cause you to make quick, and often wrong, emotional decisions about others.

Accordingly, you can potentially misunderstand your partner's feelings, behavior, and efforts. This can cause huge issues in your relationship.

By understanding your partner's attachment style better, your problems will start to smooth out, and you will be happier in your relationship.

There is one last thing we want to mention before diving into the different attachment styles. As you read through the characteristics of each of them, you might start thinking that the "best" style is the one we call the "Secure Attachment style."

That is not necessarily the case though. The "best" attachment type is the one that makes you feel safe, secure, and happy with your partner.

If you find that you're more akin to the Preoccupied Attachment style, as long as this isn't causing you or your partner any harmful repercussions, and your partner is willing to accommodate you, then that will be the "best" attachment style for you.

If your attachment style is causing you mental or physical harm, you can always strive to adopt certain aspects of the Secure Attachment Style.

The ultimate goal here is a happy, healthy, long-lasting relationship.

1.4 Happiness in Love

Sasha is fundamentally a jolly and lively person. She cherishes her work as a primary school teacher and knows she's great at it. In her free time, Sasha loves playing tennis and going on hikes with her close friends. She is also happily engaged to Tim, whom she trusts and depends on for help without hesitation.

Their relationship isn't perfect, though. For example, there was that one time Tim forgot they had made plans for dinner and basically stood her up.

Naturally, she was quite upset. But even though there are times she gets angry with him, and vice versa, they feel secure enough in the relationship to talk through their issues. Sasha knows Tim loves and cherishes her and would never do anything to cause her pain deliberately.

People with a Secure Attachment like Sasha style are confident and comfortable with the full scope of their feelings. They know that their significant other loves and understands them. They are likewise prone to thinking of their partners as reliable, good-natured, supportive, and honest. Thus, they feel free to share anything with them.

People with a Secure Attachment style offer the emotional support, loyalty, and implicit trust that their partners need.

When both you and your partner practice aspects of the Secure Attachment style, you will find yourselves in a long-lasting, steady, and healthy relationship.

Let's talk about Jack—someone you might relate to, maybe just a little bit. He always looks to his sweetheart, Agnes, for constant reassurance that he is deserving of the love and affection she gives him.

When Agnes shows Jack how important he is to her and tells him how happy she is with him, he doesn't know how to react.

He doesn't feel like he has done anything to deserve so much attention. Jack is always worried that when Agnes gets to know the "real him," she'll realize her mistake and break up with him. He also gets nervous when Agnes doesn't respond to his text messages because he thinks she's avoiding him.

This constant fear of rejection is overpowering, and it drives him into a constant state of anxiety. People like Jack have what we call the Preoccupied Attachment style.

This means that they are always fearful of the possibility of being disregarded or dismissed by their partner.

As a result, they tend to use hyper-activating techniques to keep their relationship

framework "turned on" (or active). This means that they are likely to overreact to certain situations to keep their relationship going, and thus keep a solid figure in their lives that they can attach to.

For example, say Agnes has been busy all day and hasn't had a chance to text Jack back. Jack may blow this issue out of proportion by pointing out all the times in the past that Agnes has failed to text him back. He wants her to understand that it hurts him when she doesn't reply and wants to keep that from happening in the future.

This could put unfair pressure on Agnes, who isn't actively avoiding Jack, but is only busy and wants to focus on other areas of her life.

If Jack doesn't make an effort to work on his anxiety issues, and Agnes doesn't make an effort to understand Jack, the relationship is doomed to fail.

People with Preoccupied Attachment style are highly sensitive to any potential indicators that their significant other doesn't love them anymore. This creates misunderstandings and can deeply damage their bond. Taken to an extreme, their significant other will begin to see that no amount of affection will ever be good enough and decide to end the relationship.

Although individuals with a Preoccupied Attachment style often start a relationship by feeling excited about their new love, they frequently become plagued by anxiety and distress. This causes them to be possessive and jealous to the extreme. To make matters worse, they might also turn out to be incapable of forgiving their partners for any bad behaviors, real or perceived.

People who display this attachment style often have a hard time handling problems in their social and professional lives as well.

Because they need plenty of reassurance to feel stable, their lives revolve around proving that they're deserving of success, or trying to

fend off their own negative perceptions about themselves. This interferes with their capacity to communicate with other people in a way that isn't self-sabotaging. For example, people who are anxious and apprehensive may end up bringing their personal issues and problems to the workplace. Moreover, the consistent pressure and anxiety they feel often damages their mental and physical health.

Similarly, people with a Preoccupied Attachment style approach their sexual relationships intending to gain reassurance and approval from

their significant other. They might also maintain a strategic distance from them in order to avoid rejection. So even though they frequently appreciate being held and touched, they tend to see sex as a way to obtain the desired responses of happiness and satisfaction from their partner.

Now, meet Jon. Consider whether you relate to him or if he resembles someone you know. Jon is satisfied with his freedom, his independence, and his job. He was happy with his ex, Martin, but he wasn't terribly heartbroken when Martin decided to end the relationship. Martin used to call or text Jon even when he was at work, and would often want to talk about their relationship and his feelings. Jon is actually a little relieved now that the relationship is over.

Although he sometimes feels lonely when his friends discuss their partners, Jon claims it doesn't bother him too much.

The truth is, Jon is very adept at denying his own feelings and desires, even to himself.

This trait is what defines people with a Dismissing Attachment style.

Like those with a Preoccupied Attachment style, those with a Dismissing style are likewise inclined to accept that their partners

won't dependably be there to help or comfort them.

They secure themselves by utilizing deactivating techniques that "turn off" (or deactivate) their relationship framework, enabling them to keep from being in the dreaded position of having to depend on their partner.

They adequately suppress, maintain a strategic distance from, or turn down their feelings and attachment needs.

Generally, they remain unavailable, limit their collaborations with other people, steer clear of conflict, and avoid their partners for no apparent reason. For instance, while Jon frequently appeared to be caring as he helped Martin with practical issues, such as his finances, he never offered any emotional support. In fact, Jon would always prefer to keep a safe distance from Martin whenever he got "too emotional." This caused a lot of self-confidence and self-esteem issues in Martin, which is why he ultimately decided to break up with Jon.

But people with a Dismissive Attachment style are not devoid of love.

The truth is that they do feel love for their significant other—that's why they're in a relationship with them in the first place. But their way of showing love and affection can come off as cold and uncaring.

Without understanding their own emotions, Dismissive people just aren't equipped to deal with their feelings or past traumas. For example, when their partners do something that irritates them, they will try to deny or hide their anger. But the anger is there, hiding just beneath the surface, causing them stress and anxiety.

Remaining detached will undoubtedly take its toll on the relationship, especially if your partner does not have this attachment style.

1.5 Conflicted in Love

Melanie has always thought of herself as an emotionally weak person. She had a rough childhood. Her father struggled with alcohol

problems, and her mother worked several jobs to keep the family afloat. She considers herself imperfect, needy, vulnerable, empty, and lonely and is always seeking love and affection. Although she wants to build a relationship with someone, she mostly keeps to herself and spends most of her time alone. She fears people will judge her, think her weak, and decide she's not worth their time.

This contention between intense fear of rejection and a desperate need for love, intimacy, and reassurance leads to a Fearful Attachment Style.

When people with this style of attachment meet someone new and begin a romantic relationship without overcoming their psychological issues, the relationship will likely be problematic and full of anxiety and pain.

To keep their partners close, they will exaggerate the extent of their problems. However, this behavior will mostly be completely unconscious.

When they do manage to get the attention of their significant other, a different kind of anxiety will plague their hearts—the fear that their partner will hurt them or leave them. This constant pressure causes them distress, insecurity, and loneliness and makes them inaccessible to the people around them. This will only make their anxiety and depression levels even worse.

Because they believe they're a heavy burden on their significant others, people with Fearful Attachment style often think that their partners are unwilling to maintain the relationship. This will eventually cause problems between the couple.

For example, when Melanie and her girlfriend, Georgie, started dating, they often met after work. Melanie would try to be affectionate toward Georgie, but Georgie, who had had a very difficult day at work, was stressed out and distant. Melanie will most likely believe she did something wrong and blame herself for Georgie's cold behavior. Instead of talking to Georgie about it,

Melanie, like most individuals with a Fearful Attachment style, will hide her feelings instead of talking about it to her partner.

Because of their love for their significant other, people with this attachment style will choose to stay in the relationship, even when it causes them great pain and psychological damage.

Whether their partner genuinely cares for them or not isn't the issue. The real problem is what they perceive through the lens of their anxiety disorder and past traumas.

Similarly, as they struggle with being emotionally intimate with their partners, they likewise struggle with being physically intimate. Once in a while, this implies using casual sex to address their need for comfort, acknowledgment, and consolation.

They might do this with a one-night stand or short-term relationships (that typically ends when they start feeling fearful). When they need more emotional reassurance than a physical connection, they're more likely to avoid sexual intimacy.

1.8 Styles of Attachment

If you have not done any previous research on the different types of relationship attachments, take the time to reflect on your personality and past relationships. Ready through the four styles carefully as often as you need and try to identify which one best fits you. Keep in mind that people often display characteristics of more than one attachment style.

For example, you might be a fundamentally secure person but sometimes can't help but question your self-worth when you're in a romantic relationship.

Or maybe you used to be on the needier side with a past partner, but your current partner makes you feel so loved that you're suddenly more confident and secure in your relationship.

Another great way you can visually identify your attachment style is to draw a chart like the one shown in Figure 1.

Low Avoidance

Low

Anxiety   High Anxiety

High Avoidance

Next, make even marks along both lines so that you have ten

evenly-spaced markings on the vertical and the horizontal lines.

Third, number the horizontal line, with 0 being Low Anxiety and 10 being High Anxiety. Now do the same to the vertical line, with 0 being Low Avoidance and 10 being High Avoidance.

Take the time to read through the attachment styles again and ask

yourself the following questions: In my past relationships, how would

I rate my anxiety level? In my past relationships, how would I rate my avoidance level? Do I tend to feel insecure and act needy in my relationships? Or do I choose to keep my distance from my partner?

Do I share my feelings openly, or do I come off as cold and closed-off?

Based on your self-analysis, draw an X on whatever number you feel you come closest to in the Avoidance/ Anxiety scale.

This visual exercise will help you have a clear idea of your attachment style and your tendencies when you're in a relationship. Of course, you have to be honest with yourself! Don't worry, no one has to see your results but you.

Similarly, you can try to make a separate chart for your past partners by using your perception of them and their behaviors. If you're currently in a relationship, you can ask your partner to make their own chart.

It will be a fun experience that you can do together, and you will even get to know one another even better.

You will be able to identify your areas of weakness and strength in your relationship

Chapter 2: Why Anxiety Can Take Over Your Relationship

In this fast-paced world we live in, anxiety and stress have become an increasingly prevalent part of the human condition. Mental illnesses like depression and anxiety disorders have taken over humanity without any discrimination.

Men and women of all ages have become prey to these seemingly unstoppable monsters.

The sad reality is that more and more people are becoming victims of these disorders from a very young age. High expectations from parents and teachers, and even peers, can lead to anxiety and depression in children and teenagers.

As we grow older, finding a job that pays well enough to support ourselves becomes a priority and, in most cases, our number one source of stress. To make matters worse, the pressure a lot of people feel to get married and start a family also becomes a factor that contributes to mental disorders.

Many people also have to deal with social anxiety, which means that

they will experience stress, destabilizing thoughts, and extreme insecurity when meeting other people. The outside world can be truly terrifying to people suffering from this disorder. Someone who has never had to live with anxiety or experienced an anxiety attack will never really understand what it's like for people who suffer from social anxiety.

They might dismiss your symptoms as just nerves or shyness. However, it is crucial that you do not take your anxiety disorder, or your partner's, lightly.

Whenever you feel the symptoms of an anxiety disorder, or notice them in your partner, immediately consult with your doctor to get timely treatment.

You should keep in mind that social anxiety can play really nasty tricks on your perception of the world and other people. Thoughts of inadequacy, the feeling that you're making a fool of yourself, or thinking that people are talking about you behind your back are all the result of this insidious disorder.

Since anxiety is the result of fear, confronting your fears in a safe environment is one of the best techniques of overcoming these kinds of disorders.

While some people might suggest that you simply avoid situations

that cause you stress and anxiety, the sad reality is that this is not always possible. If you suffer from social anxiety, you know how difficult it is to try to live your life if you're trying to avoid social

situations or places where many people gather. It's virtually impossible. That's why talk-therapy or Cognitive Behavioral Therapy (CBT) are vital tools for overcoming anxiety disorders. They give you the change to find the root of your fears and confront them in a safe environment.

These types of therapy are all about changing your mindset—adjusting your perceptions of what happens around you.

For example, let's consider a person who experiences an anxiety attack whenever they go into a crowded coffee shop. Such an attack will likely happen abruptly, without giving the person the chance to realize it's happening. They will be overpowered by a paralyzing fear that will trigger all sorts of physical sensations. These will, in turn, continue to feed into their fear. It's an endless, terrifying loop.

To overcome this, the socially anxious person, with the help of a professional, would have to analyze the reason for this outburst. It will take some time, but throughout their therapy session, the person will slowly begin to change their reaction to being in crowded places because they will have changed their perception of danger in such situations.

CBT has also shown excellent results in treating people with the following issues.

- Agoraphobia. The World Health Organization (WHO)

characterizes agoraphobia as the fear associated with venturing out from home, entering shops, being in groups and open places, and traveling alone on public transportation or airplanes.

Agoraphobia can regularly prompt the person to maintain an increasing distance from the circumstances and places that cause fear. For example, only venturing outside when they have a close friend or family member with them, or ordering groceries online rather than going to the store.

- Obsessive-Compulsive Behavior (OCD). OCD, like many

other anxiety disorders, can have the power to take over a person's life. The intensity of OCD varies from person to person, but the core symptoms remain the same. Unwanted, intrusive thoughts, images, or urges trigger extremely distressing feelings that make it very difficult for them to carry on with their day-to-day lives. This can further lead to depression or cause a nervous breakdown. People suffering from this problem need immediate psychological help. In the most severe cases, the individual will be unable to leave their home or might even have to undergo hospitalization. This disorder, like many anxiety disorders, often goes untreated

due to a lack of awareness. It is vital that people who suffer from this disorder, or who know people who have it, maintain open communication lines with their loved ones and physicians.

• Unwarranted Irritability. Individuals suffering from anxiety disorders often lose control of themselves and their actions. Heightened irritability is one of the most common symptoms of anxiety disorders, along with increased heart rate, sweat, muscle pain, headaches, nausea, upset stomach, and sleeping disorders. Without support and proper treatment, they will be more prone to such mood swings.

• Aggression. This is another symptom of anxiety that can cause permanent damage to a person's relationships.

When the previously mentioned irritability and mood swings turn into full-blown aggression, that's when the relationship starts to become abusive.

Aggression is sometimes a build-up from a person's childhood trauma, neglect from their loved ones, or unfair treatment from society. People with aggressive behavior are typically not very good at maintaining relationships.

If you find yourself involved with an aggressive partner, but they are not actively trying to resolve their issues, consider your options until you find the safest one for you

2.1 A Supportive Partner

Anxiety disorders are no joke and should not be treated lightly. They can be a real threat and potentially damage a person's psyche and their personal and social life.

If you have never experienced it, it can be tough to witness someone having an anxiety attack. Particularly when you don't have any idea of how the other person is feeling or what you can do to help. How you respond to the situation can either exacerbate or alleviate the intensity of the other person's attack.

That's why you must never judge a person dealing with anxiety disorders or make light of the situation. If the person is undergoing a severe attack, judgment and negativity can make the situation worse.

Although you might feel powerless watching someone have a panic attack, who might just be somebody you care about, there is nothing you can do to change how they feel at that moment.

The best solution is to be patient and quiet and stay close to the person. Try calmly asking if there's anything you can do to help.

If the attack doesn't subside or seems to be getting worse, take the person to the nearest hospital or contact their treating physician. Never give any drugs (prescribed or illegal) to anybody experiencing an anxiety or panic attack, except for the medication they have been directly prescribed by their treating physician.

These steps are the most important thing you can do for yourpartner. It might not sound like anything extraordinary, but it isprecisely what is required at that moment. Sufficient support from

loved ones can help a person in overcoming an anxiety disorder.

With the correct prescription and guidance, the individual can carry

on with an ordinary life by defeating the monster that is an anxiety

disorder.

• Take a vacation together: Stress is one of the main factors that can trigger anxiety symptoms. One of the best ways to reduce stress is to divert your mind from your daily routine. If you and your partner feel exhausted and stressed because of life's demands, it might be time to take a well-deserved break.

Planning a vacation together can help ease a lot of pressure. It doesn't have to be anything extravagant. Even a single weekend at a bed and breakfast away from home could make a world of difference.

The point is to take a break from your hectic routine and spend some time alone together. This will help you to understand each other in a better way and grow even closer. Our minds and bodies are not designed to work 24/7. So, going on vacation is a healthy and effective way to reduce stress and anxiety caused by an excessive workload.

• Visit your hometown together: Bonds of love and affection become naturally stronger the more your partner gets to know you

and vice versa. This includes your culture, family background, important places of your childhood, or meeting your friends and family members. If possible, take a short trip to each other's hometowns together. Show your partner around your old neighborhood and ask them to show you theirs.

It can be a really wonderful way to spend time together, and of understanding each other better.

- Share hobbies: Probably one of the very first things you will ask a potential romantic partner is, "What do you like to do for fun?" Or "What are your hobbies?" Something along those lines.

We mentioned before that sometimes people hide their interests for fear of rejection by the object of their affection. Some people might even lie and say they share the other person's hobbies just to seem like a better fit for them.

This definitely not an advisable way to start a relationship.

Your hobbies are an integral part of yourself. They are what bring you joy and peace in times of stress, and may even be what you go to to escape an anxiety attack or depressive period.

So if you're embarking in a new relationship, be completely honest about the things you like to do in your free time. This gives your partner a better insight into your true self and can even strengthen your bond later on. Sharing your hobbies openly with someone else can be a great ice-breaker on a first date. Remember also to pay close attention to your partner's interests. This is a two-way street, after all!

- Show interest in them: Many people love to be cared for and acknowledged by their significant other. If your partner is the type who likes to receive this kind of attention, try checking in with them when you have the time. Remember that a lack of communication is one of the leading causes of misunderstandings in a relationship. So a short phone call, text, or voice message to let them know you're thinking about them can go a long way!

• Spend quality time together: Now that you know each other's hobbies, why not enjoy them together? Watch your partner's favorite movies or teach them how to cook.

Other things you can do to spend quality time together is enjoy a long walk, a home-cooked meal, or a meaningful conversation about the things you like or dislike, or your

dreams for the future. Go to the movies, to your favorite restaurants or shopping. Sharing each other's interests will only make your bond stronger.

• Be honest: Nobody likes to be lied to. When it comes to relationships of any kind, lies are a surefire way to damage and even end the relationship. The building blocks of a healthy and long-lasting relationship are honesty and openness.

If you want to build a stable relationship with your partner, refrain hiding things from them or keeping secrets. The more you share things with your partner, the more trust and love you will get from them. When lies start surfacing in a relationship, that's when problems begin to arise.

Especially when your partner catches on to the fact that you're not being

truthful. When people start doubting their partners, they start avoiding them, which might ultimately lead to a break-up.

Chapter 3: How to change yourself to reduce the toxicity in your relationships

Your personality and identity are the aspects of yourself that you can rely on each day to help you navigate the intricacies of life.

Like the ground beneath your feet, they support every aspect of your existence. Whenever you look in the mirror, you know who is looking back.

Even though we all change as we grow older, you know yourself better than anyone else.

However, people with self-image issues or anxiety disorders may not be as secure in their own identity. They can't see the parts of themselves that are worthy, and their mental health suffers as a result.

When people successfully identify the valuable aspects of their personality, they are better able to stay positive and view life with a clear and confident perspective.

This fills the person with determination, motivation, and a more positive outlook on life. This is why self-confident people tend to have successful relationships.

On the other hand, a person who lives in a constant state of self-doubt and self-deprecation will be unmotivated and indecisive.

Their minds will be plagued with negative thoughts. They will live an unhappy life, likely unable to form bonds that are healthy and nurturing.

It is essential to remain alert to the kind of vibe you give off to the

people around you and the vibe they give off in exchange. By paying close attention to other people's words and actions, you might develop a "sixth sense" for their real personality. This will help you determine whether they are someone you want to invest your time and energy on.

Suppose you start a relationship without knowing what the other person is really like. This can potentially lead to an unhealthy

relationship when you realize how incompatible you are later on down the road.

Now that you know about attachment styles, keep an eye on your potential romantic partner's behavior, then decide if it's worth pursuing a deeper relationship.

We have already talked about the Preoccupied Attachment style. You probably remember that people with this attachment style have a high level of both anxiety and attachment. They tend to become extremely attached to their partners and remain in a constant state of anxiousness and worry.

They live in continuous fear that their partner will leave them and thus come off as needy.

Remember the Dismissing Attachment style? This is where the avoidant partner keeps themselves at a safe distance from their significant other to avoid being emotionally compromised.

Now imagine that a person with a Preoccupied Attachment style starts dating someone with a Dismissing Attachment style. There is absolutely no compatibility in the way these two people express love and affection for their romantic partners.

Moreover, their needs are entirely different.

When the preoccupied person notices the avoidant person's behavior, they will start to believe that the avoidant partner is not interested anymore and will leave soon. On the other hand, the avoidant partner won't understand what the problem is. They think it's evident that they care for their partner, and don't think they need to be openly affectionate to prove their love.

As you can probably imagine, if these two don't meet each other halfway, the relationship will only end in disaster.

So, before starting a relationship, it is always better to know yourself and your attachment style, as well as the other person's. This also goes for couples who have been together for a long time. It's never too late to discover these fundamental aspects of your significant other's personality.

The way you see yourself and others play a crucial role in your relationships. The older we grow, and the more people we meet, our brain creates a sort of database for different personality types. This database provides a picture or idea based on our style and preferences of what we require from our romantic partners.

When we meet someone new, we instinctively look into this database to see if they match our needs. Typically, we only get a small amount of evidence that other is right for us based on the image that they intentionally project. This image may or may not be the true extent of their personality.

That's why it is so important to get to know the other person beyond our initial impression of them.

If we take the example of people with a Preoccupied Attachment style, we can see this very clearly. It may be the case that when they first start a relationship, they will be happy and satisfied with their new romance.

However, as time goes on, they may start to think that their partner will cheat on them and leave.

If this is not addressed, the more time passes, those fears will only grow and begin to seep into the foundations of the relationship. Whether the other person will really cheat or not, the insecure person will be haunted by these negative thoughts, and the relationship will most likely end, which is exactly what they predicted in the first place.

Psychologists use the term "confirmation bias" for this phenomenon. This term is used to describe people's tendency to look for ways to verify their thoughts and beliefs, whether it's the truth or not. The term self-verification is used when people successfully verify their beliefs by altering reality to fit their thoughts.

These processes of confirmation bias and self-verification are the opposite of awareness and knowledge. They mostly cause distress and pain.

People aren't always aware that they're doing it, though. As a result, these unseen biased perceptions make a person repeat old behaviors and patterns, even though they always lead to frustration and agony.

If handled properly, constantly failing in life and ending up alone in relationships can potentially lead to people questioning their beliefs and biases.

They can become more open and receptive to change and to improve their lives ultimately.

Let's talk once more about the anxiously attached person from our previous example. This person is always insecure in relationships, but never understands what goes wrong and ultimately ends the relationship.

By doing some truthful and honest soul-searching, this person may discover that their biases and fearful mindset are the cause of all their problems.

When this person puts aside their biases and beliefs, they may become more open to loving and trusting people.

Trusting other people comes from a place of self-love. When you trust other people, it's because you know you're worthy of love.

When people experience some kind of attachment-related anxiety, then opening up to the possibility that they are valuable and worthy of love is very important. This self-confidence will lead to successful, healthy, and nurturing relationships.

Eliminating the tendency to self-verify and view life through the lens of confirmation bias is challenging. It is a process that can only begin when we take an honest look at the most profound aspects of ourselves and are willing to make a change.

3.1 See Yourself in a different way

You can change your way of thinking and even your attachment style when you stop practicing self-verification. Once you know what your biases are and realize how unrealistic and harmful they are, you will gain a new perspective. You will become aware of when you experience an unrealistic fear of rejection or when you're being unnecessarily self-critical.

With enough work and effort, you will slowly but surely begin to eliminate these beliefs and biases from your life. They will be replaced by positive and practical thoughts, which will, in turn, contribute to having healthier relationships.

It can be difficult at first, though. This new mindset can feel alien and even wrong since you're so used to always fearing the worst. You will most likely question these new positive thoughts and their credibility. The reason behind this is that they challenge the very foundation of who you perceive yourself to be and the foundation of your relationship. This can really upset a person's sense of comfort and wellbeing. Gradually, though, you will be able to see yourself and your partner in a new and different way.

3.2 Do You really Know Yourself?

Our perception of ourselves plays an essential role in determining whether we believe we are worthy of love or not.

We categorize ourselves and "worthy and loveable" or "unworthy and unlovable."

This self-verification is done by using three methods: selective attention, selectively interpreting information, and selective memory. These methods tend to overlap and lead to the same results—being worthy or being unworthy.

Selective attention means that we tend to pay more attention to feedback that confirms our existing lovability or unlovability belief.

Selectively interpreting information means that any piece of information we receive about our worth will be altered in our minds to fit our self-perception. It also means that we tend to believe in such feedback without any questions or second thoughts.

Selective memory means that we only remember words, events, or situations that confirm our sense of being unworthy or worthy of love.

People who face attachment-related anxiety selectively confirm and self-verify that they are not worthy of love. They tend to remember things their past or present partners said that lower their self-esteem or make them feel flawed. Meanwhile, they fail to recognize the times their partners appreciated them or stood by them in a tough time.

3.3 Observe Yourself

Hopefully, by now, you have identified your attachment style, as well as your level of attachment-related anxiety. That will help you to determine your self-perception of worthiness.

We will now ask you some questions that will help you better understand how you maintain the self-perception of being worthy or unworthy of love. This step is crucial and, if answered honestly, will help you break out of a toxic cycle of insecurity and anxiety.

This can be done with your partner or anyone you feel safe and close with. The exercise can be repeated every day until you get to the root of the issues you are facing.

We suggest that you write down your answers to keep a visual guide and stay focused. Hold on to your answers, because they will be crucial for the exercise in the next chapter.

If you're doing this exercise with someone, keep an open line of communication with them, and remain open to what they have to say. The perspective of someone who knows you well can be a precious resource.

When's the first time you remember feeling you weren't worthy of love?

What were the circumstances leading to you feeling unworthy?

You will likely remember many such situations. Try to recall as

far back as you can, to the earliest years of your childhood.

What was your reaction to the events that made you feel unworthy? Were you confused, uncomfortable, sad?

Now try remembering your reaction to more recent situations when you felt unworthy.

Are you making assumptions based on what you think the other person is thinking about you? Are jumping to conclusions without asking the other person what they really think?

Suppose the other person did say something that you perceive as negative. Do you minimize the negative feedback or dismiss it? Or do you start second-guessing yourself and doubting the other person's love for you?

Now let's move onto selective memory. Think of everything you did today. Big or small, it doesn't matter, everything counts.

In what ways did your family, friends, or colleagues show appreciation for you?

Did your partner do anything to show their love for you? If the answer is yes, then in what ways?

What about last week? Last month?

If you can't find the answers to these questions, or you believe that no one around you displays any affection for you, you may be engaging in selective memory behavior.

Finally, the following exercise will challenge your selective interpretation of information.

Do you often think that the people around you dismiss you or criticize you based on an off-comment or gesture?

This could mean you're misinterpreting the other person's intentions with very little or no evidence. Maybe you misread the other person's tiredness as saying that you are uninteresting.

Do you often criticize your abilities and minimize your strengths?

Maybe you're comparing yourself against other people, and your expectations are way too unrealistic.

Take your time to think about your answers to all the above questions.

Observe how you employ self-verification and conformation bias when you think about yourself, selective attention, interpretation, and memory.

Do you see any repeating behaviors or patterns? What kind of attitude do you see in yourself?

Some behaviors and attitudes you may recognize in yourself are jealousy, fear of rejection, feelings of unworthiness, low self-esteem, etc.

You often think that you're flawed, inadequate, or not as amazing and wonderful as your friends or significant other.

You also frequently think that your partner will stop loving you if they see the "real" you.

Just as we unconsciously use confirmation bias to self-verify how worthy or unworthy of love we are, we also use it to get a sense of how emotionally available or unavailable our partner is. We also use it during our interactions with friends and colleagues.

People who already think that others will not be there for them in a time of need are more emotionally insecure. They tend to see their partners as emotionally unavailable and inaccessible. This makes them to feel alone and abandoned. In turn, they protect themselves by being self-supporting and self-reliant.

You may initially be happy and positive at the beginning of your relationship, but your perceptions will turn negative over time. As mentioned before, you may start thinking that your partner is not loyal.

Everything they do and say will turn into hints that will convince you that your partner will leave you soon.

If your partner doesn't return your call, it must be because they don't care about you. The

idea that maybe they're extremely busy with work doesn't even cross your mind.

And so, without any concrete evidence, you will jump to the conclusion that your partner doesn't love you and is disloyal.

This mostly happens to people with Preoccupied or Fearful Attachment styles. Even a small trigger will make things worse, and any little inconvenience will be enough to start a fight.

However, if you take the time to work on yourself and address your insecurity issues, you are much more likely to have a happy relationship with fewer misconceptions.

This can best be explained by looking at Elias and Annabelle's relationship. Elias constantly mocks and ridicules Annabelle's love of knitting.

Annabelle never set boundaries, but instead avoided knitting in front of Elias to keep from being ridiculed. Eventually, she stopped knitting altogether.

This behavior makes Elias feel superior and reinforces the usefulness of mocking Annabelle to control her. In turn, Annabelle stops doing the things she loves when Elias starts making fun of her for it. This kind of behavior is called a "closed-loop relationship."

When two people in a relationship perpetuate the loop—for example, when Annabelle keeps avoiding the activities she likes because Elias keeps ridiculing her—this will only reinforce each person's perception of each other and their relationship.

Even though the relationship could turn toxic and harmful, people will rarely choose to leave their partners. This is because such predictable pattern gives the two people involved a sense of safety and security. They know exactly how to react and how their partner will react, and what to expect from their partners and from themselves. This sense of predictability can be very comforting.

Even if the behavior is painful or humiliating, as long as it fulfills your self-perception, it's okay.

This is especially the case for people with low self-esteem and anxiety disorders. They often choose to surround themselves with people that are less supportive and reinforce their sense of being unworthy.

This makes people with low self-esteem stay in toxic relationships instead of looking for nurturing, loving partners. Some people may even be utterly blind to the abuse.

It is only with therapy, the appropriate medication, and a lot of

introspection that people who suffer from these disorders are able to

change themselves and develop new relationships. In the transition

from low self-esteem to unconditional self-love, some old relationships may start to change for the better. More often than not, however, the most toxic of relationships will come to an end.

When you cut ties with the toxic people in your life, you're room for new relationships that will nurture you "new self.'" Acknowledging and accepting the need for change ahead of the time will make this transition easier for you.

The scenario mentioned above can also be explained by taking the example of the movie Pretty Woman. If we critically observe Edward (Richard Gere's character), we'll see he's a strong, accomplished, and successful businessman. However, his approach to life is cold and dismissive of other people's feelings. Then he meets Vivian (Julia Roberts' character), who challenges his way of thinking and pushes him to open up.

At first, he was hesitant to change, but eventually, he becomes a warmer person with open and encouraging emotions. His professional life was also positively affected by this change, as he started treating the people he worked with more humanely.

3.4 The Most Common Problem in a Relationship

Now we're going to talk about something called the "pursuit-withdrawal pattern." This toxic behavior is sadly very common in relationships. It mostly emerges between an avoidant partner and an anxiously-attached partner. If you have ever been part of such a dynamic, chances are you have experienced the pursuit-withdrawal pattern.

The easiest way to explain it is that the attached person in a

relationship continually tries to show affection, while the avoidant partner tends to pull away.

This causes the anxious partner to show even more love in an attempt to get closer to their significant other, who then becomes even more closed off and distant.

Finding intimacy in such a dynamic is very hard, if not downright impossible.

Let's use the example of Helen and Michael. After successfully dating for a year, they decided to move in together.

Unfortunately, after some time, their relationship started to face some problems. Michael expected Helen to give him undivided attention and love.

Meanwhile, when Helen asks Michael for help doing chores, he always says that Helen does a better job and he would only get in the way.

Thus, Helen always ends up doing everything herself.

Their dynamic becomes the following. Michael is never satisfied with the amount of attention Helen gives him. In turn, Helen may become more withdrawn. Helen is also angry because Michael doesn't help her with the chores.

In turn, Michael, who doesn't handle anger well, becomes more submissive and tries to show Helen more affection.

They both believe they're putting their best effort to keep the relationship going. Still, they each end up feeling unsatisfied.

Michael, being the anxiously attached partner, craves attention and love. But Helen, being the avoidant partner, fails to fulfill Michael's needs.

Both sides of this relationship are common and easy to understand.

Often, we want to feel a connection with someone, but the other person is unable to reciprocate.

On the other hand, maybe sometimes we feel overwhelmed by our partner's need for attention and wish they would help out with the more practical aspects of a relationship.

Michael needs constant reassurance to feel loved, and Helen's avoidant reaction makes him feel insecure. This pushes Helen into a state of perpetual annoyance and becomes demanding of Michael's help with chores.

Michael doesn't understand Helen's coldness. Due to her unresponsiveness, negative thoughts emerge in his mind, and he becomes needier. He fails to see the pressure this puts on Helen.

When an avoidant person like Helen faces this kind of situation, they prefer to maintain a safe distance in order to avoid conflict. They tend to develop an emotionally safe distance.

Avoidant people feel more comfortable when they are independent. They don't like to feel vulnerable, especially when other people demand more attention from them. This only makes them withdraw even further.

As is to be expected, both of the people involved in this dynamic will have different thoughts about their relationship.

The thoughts of anxiously-attached people run something along the lines of how their partners would love them if they were smarter or more attractive. How every problem that arises in the relationship is their fault. How their significant other must be angry with them since they aren't returning their calls.

We don't spend enough time together. My partner probably doesn't care about my feelings. They're never around, and they didn't get me anything for my birthday. We haven't gone on a date in forever. They're probably going to break up with me soon.

Does any of this sound familiar? These are all constant thoughts that plague the mind of an anxiously-attached person.

On the other hand, the thoughts of an avoidant partner are focused on maintaining a safe distance.

I always try to do what my partner wants, but it never seems to be enough. Nothing I do is ever right. I can't figure out how to make them happy. They get upset easily so I don't want to talk about our problems and get into a fight. It's better if I change the subject, I don't want to get into it with them right now.

These thoughts might lead the avoidant person to think that they're better off alone since they can't seem to make their partner happy.

The longer the pursuit-attachment dynamic goes on unaddressed, the more extreme and toxic the situation will become. After a few years of this, the avoidant person could become more hostile and completely closed-off, while the anxious partner can become severely depressed and lonely.

No matter how hard the anxious partner tries to get love, attention, and warmth from the avoidant partner, nothing works.

The avoidant partner becomes aggressive, which is mainly passive aggression, expressed through cold silence, being disrespectful, and rolling eyes.

There are many reasons why people choose to remain in relationships like this. As mentioned before, the predictability could be a source of comfort, however harmful it may be. Maybe whenever one or the other person is about to end the relationship, they remember the good times and realize that they really do love the

other person. Or maybe it's just a matter of habit—they're so used to being together that they can't see the relationship ending.

However, it is also not uncommon for the anxious partner to get tired of being the only one who is emotionally involved and deciding to end the relationship.

You should pay attention to the patterns of communication in your relationship. Keenly observe which of those patterns lead to conflicts and fights. To do this, you should keep a close eye on your partner's actions, words, thoughts, and feelings.

If we look at Helen and Michael's example again, we will see that one of Michael's main problems is that Helen doesn't spend time with him on weekends. Instead, she chooses to catch up on work or spend time with her friends. This makes Michael feel lonely and unworthy of love. He tried talking to Helen about this and ended up crying and calling Helen selfish.

On the other hand, Helen feels that Michael is being too emotional. She deals with the situation by distancing herself from him, which hurts Michael more, and the cycle continues.

Now think of the fight or conflicts that often repeat in your relationship.

Keep that in mind as you answer the following questions.

As the conflict is happening, how do you feel about the whole situation?

What do you think about your partner?

How do you try to resolve the problem?

Now think about your partner.

How does your partner feel on the receiving end?

What is your partner telling you about their perception of you?

How does your partner tend to respond to what you have to say?

Next, observe how the conflict usually ends. Does it end in withdrawal? Or in an explosion of anger and accusations?

If you feel comfortable, try answering these questions with your partner. Remember to remain respectful of what your partner has to say. Try putting yourself in their shoes and really understand where they're coming from. Ask them to do the same for you.

3.5 Be Aware of Your Patterns

Now that you've answered all these questions about your attachment style and recurring behaviors, you're likely starting to become aware of your patterns in relationships.

If you and your partner feel comfortable and relaxed, the next step is to try having a conversation about the previous exercises. Here are some questions you can answer with your partner.

How do you feel after you have a problematic interaction or fight?

Are you both emotionally available for each other?

How do you affect each other's feelings?

How do you react to how the other person is feeling?

What behavior patterns did you notice in yourselves and each other?

What is the influence of the patterns on your relationship?

Try keeping these questions in mind as you have this conversation. They will help identify and smooth out your differences. To summarize, this chapter has helped you learn about how you form attachments, your attachment style.

We also talked about confirmation bias and self-verification, which contribute to you repeating old and sometimes harmful patterns. They tend to deceive and distort your perceptions. You need to take an in-depth look at how you have dealt with your past relationships to overcome these habits.

The next chapter will discuss how having an abstract idea of how to manage problems isn't enough. You need to be able to implement practical solutions to your everyday life to overcome obstacles.

You will learn how to use practical tools to break your toxic patterns and establish and maintain healthier and happier relationships.

Chapter 4: Overcome Obstacles in Your Relationship

After you've been in a relationship for some time, you tend to develop a good idea of the issues you face as a couple. In an ideal world, we would address these issues with our partner, and our relationship would remain happy and healthy.

But let's be honest. That is nowhere near as easy as it sounds.

For example, people sometimes get jealous and unconsciously do things that can hurt their partners. Rather than talk to their significant other, they develop a lack of trust and start invading their partner's personal space or privacy.

It is neither uncommon nor a bad sign that you have fights with your partner. It's only what's expected after spending a lot of time with another person. How to solve these problems is the real heart of the issue, though. It can be challenging, but with enough patience, you and your partner will be able to overcome the obstacles in your relationship. Here are some ways you can accomplish this.

Maintaining an open line of communication with your partner can help you grow closer and strengthen your bond. Paradoxically, one of the main problems couples face is lack of communication.

Communicating is fairly difficult at the start of the relationship. Because people are focused on making a good impression, they often don't set clear boundaries and are afraid of being open with their love romantic interest. However, the beginning of a relationship is precisely the right moment to set boundaries and be honest about your needs and expectations.

Even though it might be difficult and leave you feeling vulnerable, the best advice we can give is to communicate your needs to your new partner right off the bat.

That way, when you've been together for a while, your partner will be able to understand your behavior patterns and vice versa.

You have an open mind and open communication rather than sending out cryptic messages for your partner to decipher. When you're only just getting to know someone, this obscure communication can lead to misunderstandings and misinterpretations. One of the best ways to overcome poor communication is to ask your partner for clarification before jumping to your own conclusions.

Always keep in mind that communication is one of the fundamental pillars of a relationship. Sooner or later, you will have to master the art of communication with your partner, so doesn't it make sense to get started on it as early on in the relationship as possible?

As you might expect, when you start a new relationship, there will be some changes in your everyday life. At the start of the relationship, people tend to focus more on their partners and may even lose sight of other aspects of their lives. This is perfectly normal.

However, you should try your best not to set your expectations too high. Try to keep your feet as firmly planted on the ground as you can. Don't lose sight of the fact that your new love, regardless of how perfect they may seem, is only human and therefore has both positive and negative characteristics.

Accepting them as they are, without trying to change them, is another pillar of a healthy relationship.

You should not see your significant other as someone who will fill the void inside you. Having too many expectations from your partner can cause issues for you in the long run. A relationship is in no way a cure-all, nor should it be seen as the only solution to feelings of loneliness. This mindset can cause all kinds of problems in your current relationship.

While it is true that being with someone can bring us feelings of happiness and love, setting the bar too high can lead to disappointment and heartbreak.

Your partner should be someone who stands by your side and supports you as you navigate life and its ups and downs. Not the one who battles your demons for you. You need to understand that no one can resolve your inner conflicts except for you.

It's natural to feel a sense of security when we have someone by our side. But this shouldn't cross the line into feeling panicked when someone or something threatens to take away that security. This is the same panic that a child may feel when they think their parents might leave them.

It's not always easy to identify someone's behavior patterns and attachment style when you're just starting to get to know them. When you first meet someone, you'll probably notice only the best parts of them, the ones they put forward to make a good impression. In most cases, though, your significant other's true nature might take a long time to surface.

Imagine you're just starting a relationship with someone. It's all sunshine and happiness for the first few weeks or months. But then your partner hits a rough patch in their life. Suddenly, you notice that they're drinking a lot more than they used to. Not only that, but your partner seems to be taking out his frustrations on you. They're becoming verbally and maybe even physically abusive.

In cases such as this, many people respond with denial. They think it's probably just a temporary setback. Their partner is under a lot of stress after all, so it's only natural that they're more aggressive than usual. Their partner used to be so sweet, it's only a matter of time before they go back to how they were.

Someone outside of the relationship looking in will see how toxic and harmful this relationship has become. But the truth is, the two people involved may be so deep in their self-deception that they start seeing their situation as normal.

Many factors contribute to this type of unhealthy relationship. If one or both parties suffer from some kind of mental illness—such as depression or an anxiety disorder—getting out of toxic relationships can be tough.

This is part of the reason why we need to become more aware of mental illnesses and try to get treatment as quickly as possible.

However, you need to keep in mind that conflicts are part and parcel of any relationship, especially with two people with completely different attachment styles.

A person's early experiences tend to shape their behavior patterns in relationships. People who receive a lot of attention in their early childhood tend to be highly emotional in their future relationships. In contrast, people with absent parents or caregivers will likely present a more avoidant attachment style.

All our past experiences impact our relationships. It's the reason why we sometimes have a hard time getting along with our partners. Because most of us find it difficult to change behaviors that have been ingrained in us since childhood, we won't know how to accommodate our partner's behaviors.

Typically, people rely on other people based on their previous experiences and respond in the way that they think is best for them.

Let's look at Daisy, for example. Daisy was treated harshly by her family when she was a young girl. As an adult, she always goes out of her way to please other people, even at the expense of her own feelings and mental health. She's overly cautious around her partner, always trying to avoid upsetting them in any way. However, she never expresses her own feelings or needs.

Taking care of your partner is an essential part of a relationship. But when that turns into being afraid to upset them and neglecting yourself, that's when you know that relationship is becoming unhealthy.

Not talking to your significant other about your thoughts, feelings,

and issues will only cause a rift between you. Over time, all those problems will pile up until the relationship is destroyed beyond repair.

Couples therapy is one of the best ways to deal with such situations. It will give you the tools you need to deal with your problems before they get out of hand and potentially save your relationship.

4.1 Discover Hidden Problems In A Relationship

Now that you've learned about self-deception, it's time to talk about how to discover the hidden problems in your relationship. All human beings have emotional baggage. So, when two people with a vastly different and complex set of issues form a relationship, it can be challenging for them to function together.

One of the main issues that you are going to face with a new partner is the difference in beliefs. This is also termed as cognitive dissonance. This is a problem that can affect all kinds of relationships. When two people have different belief systems, working through their issues can be even more complicated.

There are different ways in which cognitive dissonance can affect a relationship. As we have mentioned before, people develop their attachment style to feel safe in the world and be happy with their partner.

Our childhood experiences continue to affect our adult lives, how we see ourselves, and what biases we develop. We are continually trying to prove to the world who we are. This can make things difficult if we have been avoiding serious problems all our lives.

For example, an overly-anxious person with low self-esteem is more likely to have cognitive dissonance issues and see themselves as worthless and unlovable. This person probably engages in self-verification almost constantly and is unable to see the difference between a compliment and a negative comment.

Thinking something along the lines of "it's all in the past, I should just get over it" does more harm than good in most cases of mental illness and childhood trauma.

It should be evident by now that therapy is one of the best ways to get to the root of your problems and begin a healing process.

This is also the case for people with naturally avoidant tendencies and thus outwardly seem better at handling emotional pain and instability. The truth is, they avoid such issues precisely because they're unable to deal with them.

For example, Peter was a homemaker who utilized self-control to maintain a rigorous structure for himself and his family.

As his children grew older, though, they started to challenge his meticulous restraint. He began to lose his temper more and more often. His children's developing autonomy triggered the flood of his previously smothered feelings.

Realizing the extent of his negative emotions made it impossible for him to remain serenely independent as he had been. He discovered just how alone he felt in his marriage.

He now saw how emotionally inaccessible he had been from his significant other, and that he, to some degree, had caused this rift.

The very nature of hidden or suppressed feelings makes dealing with them all the more troublesome. To be able to acknowledge and address these issues, we should continually challenge the standards of confirmation bias and self-verification we live by.

An excellent first step is to eliminate thoughts like "my partner won't love me if they

know the real me."

Let's take a look at Peter again. After his breakdown, he decided to go to therapy. He was able to recognize that he never fully confided in his partner for emotional support.

Peter felt weak whenever his partner offered help and ended up distancing himself and becoming more closed off.

When he was ready to open up about his problems and be vulnerable with his partner, Peter realized that his partner had been lonely in their relationship too, and craved a more intimate relationship with Peter.

By keeping an open mind to really getting to know yourself and other

people, you will start to let go of your grasp on the past and will finally begin to heal your old wounds.

This can help you change how you identify with yourself and other people in the present moment.

We discussed how you can discover your identity in a previous chapter. Now we will take that exercise to the next level. This will help you further understand how you use confirmation bias and self-verification.

Ask yourself the following questions:

How do you behave when you feel discomfort and stress?

How do your biases affect your behavior around other people?

Some people tend to lose control when their beliefs are challenged, which can affect their overall behavior.

For example, an insecure person may think that their partner is only

being affectionate out of obligation, rather than genuine love. But

instead of allowing yourself to continue with this line of thinking, you should make an effort to believe that your partner truly cherishes you.

Try practicing this exercise with different problems you may have with your partner. Getting into the habit of being mindful of your biases and behaviors will help you see your part in your relationship issues. It can be useful and illuminating to share your perceptions, considerations, and feelings with your significant other.

4.2 How Pain Can Change People

Emotional pain can affect people in different ways. Some people may develop depression or other mental illnesses. Anxiety, sleep deprivation, fatigue, headaches, and muscle pain are all common manifestations of emotional duress.

Many people often don't address issues associated with their mental health, though. Instead, they may turn to substance abuse, compulsive shopping, risky behavior, or overworking themselves to cope with the pain.

But these practices only provide temporary respite at best, and even more serious health problems at worst.

We have talked about how anxious and avoidant individuals deal with emotional problems in different ways. Even though avoidant people may seem more in control, the reality is that they also experience triggers that force them out of their comfort zone and cause them emotional distress. This can manifest itself in feelings of alienation from the people around them and powerlessness when forced to confront their emotions.

This means that whatever our attachment style is, we're all just human beings who experience pain, disappointment, stress, and loneliness.

It is only by facing the challenge of genuinely observing and accepting our own feelings and other people's that we will be able to form deeper connections.

4.3 Be Open to New Experiences

If you have been hurt in the past, you know how difficult it is to remain open to new experiences. Absent or neglectful parents, bullying, cheating or lying romantic partners—all these factors contribute to a person becoming more closed off and unwilling to put themselves in a position where they'll be vulnerable again.

Of course, it's only natural not to want to get hurt. But avoiding new experiences out of fear means missing out on some of the most significant moments in our lives.

You should allow yourself to be let your guard down and be vulnerable with the people you love and who love you.

This is not easy. In fact, it can be downright terrifying. But it is only by putting ourselves out there that we will have healthy and happy relationships with other people.

Don't pressure yourself to do this right away, though. This process takes a lot of time, patience, and, most importantly, self-love and understanding.

As always, let's look at a practical example. Julia's parents loved her and her siblings dearly. Anyone could see that they were a happy family.

However, Julia's parents would mostly focus on her academic accomplishments rather than offering emotional support. When Julia came home crying one day because her classmates had bullied her, her parents reacted with orders not to cry.

They told her to be strong and ignore the harassment she was facing. This was always her parents' response whenever Julia got hurt.

As she grew older, Jessie learned not to cry or express the emotions her parents deemed as "negative" or "dramatic." She started to believe that her personality was flawed and that displaying feelings of hurt meant she was weak and undeserving of her parents' love.

Her parents' constant pressure on her to be the top of her class also made her feel that regardless of her achievements, she would never be good enough.

Fearing other people would see how weak and flawed she was, she learned to smile even when she felt miserable.

As an adult, Julia is hyper-critical of herself and the impression she makes on other people. She constantly changes aspects of her personality to please the people around her.

Julia also avoids getting too close to others. She doesn't have any

friends who know the real her, and all her relationships have been

short—ended before her partner could get to know who she really was.

If Julia wants to change this, her only course of action is to take a close look at her self-perception, and what type of connections she makes with others. Once she allows herself to acknowledge her feelings, she will finally be able to make deep and meaningful bonds.

4.4 Tips to Overcome Problems in a Relationship

You and your partner have to be willing to see the problems that

arise in your relationship and learn to overcome them together.

There are many things that can cause friction between two people, causing arguments and disagreements of varying degrees of severity. Here are some ways you can both tackle these issues as they arise to prevent them from becoming even worse in the future.

4.5 Listen

If you have the habit of jumping in and interrupting your partner when they're speaking, this may be one of the main causes of your problems.

Not listening to what your significant other says can create a massive rift between you. "I feel like my partner doesn't listen to me" is actually one of the most common complaints therapists hear.

You need to listen to the partner to understand their concerns. Don't treat this expression of their feelings as a debate. Listen attentively and wait until they're finished before you interject. This way, your partner will feel appreciated and understood in a more meaningful way than, say, showering them with compliments.

Take a few deep breaths when you get an urge to talk and focus on your partner's words. Maintaining eye contact throughout the conversation is an excellent way to stay focused on them.

4.6 Avoid the blame game

When a conflict arises in a relationship, some people tend to place the blame on their partner.

While both of you need to acknowledge toxic behaviors that may have contributed to your problem, placing blame on your partner or yourself will get you nowhere.

Rather than finding faults with your partner's actions or words, the main thing you should focus on when having a discussion is how to solve the conflict. The best way to go about this is to wait until you have both calmed down. Take some time apart to examine the conflict and see it as objectively as possible. Statements like "maybe

I overreacted" or "I could have handled that better" go a long way in maintaining a calm and unbiased discussion. Remember, it takes two people to make or break a relationship. So, while you may not have the ability to change your partner, you can control how you react.

When you sit down with your partner and keep an open and honest communication, without judging each other, you will be able to solve your issues more effectively. That is the sign of a true partnership, rather than two people attacking one another while trying to protect themselves.

4.7 Spend time together

Hey, we get it. The pressures and responsibilities of being an adult don't really leave us with a lot of free time. This sometimes means that we don't have enough time to spend with our families, friends, or romantic partners.

Now be honest. Are you making the most out of the time that you do spend with your partner?

Do you take part in mutually satisfactory activities, or do you both mostly just stare at the TV or your phones?

There's nothing wrong with watching movies or TV shows together. But having this be the only kind of activity you do together might be detrimental to your relationship.

Try establishing some "us" time. Ask each other questions about your week, your ups and downs, what made you happy, or what you would like to do together.

During these conversations, abstain from looking at your phone or discussing relationship problems. If you make this a habit, your bond is sure to grow even stronger and more intimate.

4.8 Make sure you're on the same page Appreciate each other

Disagreements can really damage a relationship if not appropriately addressed. A common example of this is financial issues. It's not easy to talk about personal finances, which can often drive a wedge between you and your romantic partner. Regardless of whether you've just started dating and are trying to decide who pays for dinner or are in a serious relationship and signing up for a joint bank account, money issues can really harm a relationship.

You both must understand each other's financial situation and goals. Have candid conversations about your finances as individuals and as a couple and make sure you're on the same page. Or at least reading the same book.

This goes for your expectations from your relationship as well.

You need to know your significant other's perspective of your partner and why they take a stand on the issues that they do. Keeping an open mind can help you overcome problems at a much faster pace.

For some people, not showing acknowledgment or gratitude makes them feel underappreciated, misunderstood, and unloved. When we express our appreciation and affection for our partner, we are letting them know what we cherish and love about them. This is very important to help a relationship grow and remain stable.

Make it a habit to show your appreciation for your partner. Saying things like, "You dealt with that really well" or "you're really good at doing " goes a long way in making your partner feel loved.

Enjoy!

What's the point of being together if you don't enjoy each other's company?

Sharing things that make you happy, laughing together, and doing fun activities play a huge role in strengthening your relationship. Look into fun things to do in your neighborhood or take a weekend trip somewhere nearby. Remember to ask your partner what they like doing and make plans together!

Chapter 5: Create a Sense of Security for Your Relationship

Let's do a quick recap of what we've covered so far.

By now, you should know what your attachment style is and have a good idea of how you see and behave around your partner. You also understand that open communication is one of the most important aspects of a healthy relationship.

Additionally, you may have already started to work on setting aside unrealistic expectations of you and your partner. You're beginning to devote yourself to unconditional self-love, as well as loving and understanding your partner in every way you can. You're aware that letting go of your old behavior patterns and biases is a difficult task.

Still, patience and resilience will help you accomplish your goal.

Your new perspective will naturally cause you to understand your partner better, and it may even help you alter your relationship style.

You're probably asking yourself the following question: "How do I maintain this new perspective and avoid unhealthy patterns from resurfacing?"

When a person is presented with this question, it is essential to look

for direct and practical answers. Having concrete tools at your disposal is the best way to tackle any new conflicts that arise as you endeavor to eliminate unhealthy habits.

You're going to have to start deciding what attitudes are acceptable for your new mindset, and which ones are not. Be aware that sometimes these decisions may end up being the wrong ones. Don't be discouraged, though. Through trial and error, you will slowly but surely find the solutions that are right for you.

Also keep in mind that the definition of a happy relationship is different from person to person. If you still feel anxious or stressed in your relationship, even after all this work, that might be an indicator that your partner isn't right for you.

Remember that the more we practice self-love, the more our toxic relationships will begin to fall by the wayside. Imagine a small potted plant sitting on a desk in a windowless office. It's green leaves fill the small, dark room with warmth, but it doesn't seem to be able to grow any flowers.

Now imagine that you move this plant to a big room with huge windows and lots of sunlight. Soon after, you will surely start to see colorful blossoms popping out all over.

Not unlike this little plant, people can get the "sunlight" they need to blossom from a healthy relationship.

If you find yourself in the shadows of a "dark and windowless" relationship, but you still want to see if you can find some light in it, there are a couple of things you can do.

The first one is, of course, talking to your partner. If you don't feel ready for that, then confiding in someone close to you can be a great first step. Try talking to a relative, friend, therapist, spiritual guide, or whoever you feel comfortable with.

Another tool you might want to look into is what's called "merciful awareness."

This practice is all about developing consciousness of yourself when you feel emotional or physical distress and using that awareness to reduce your pain.

In both cases, whether from your loved ones or from your increasing self-awareness, love will make its way into your heart, providing comfort and the assurance that you are deserving of it.

In order to form stable and long-lasting relationships, you need to be able and willing to accept your partner from a place of sincere love and emotional openness.

With the help of a loving partner, you will start to see positive

changes in your life. You will change and grow with the help of your partner as you nurture your relationship. What's more, you will have a better understanding of who your significant other is, what truly matters to them, what makes them happy, and how to comfort them when they're in pain.

Next, we'll be taking an in-depth look at the two key elements needed in creating a healthy and long-lasting relationship: self-awareness and self-compassion.

5.1 Self-Awareness

As we discussed earlier, when you're in a relationship, it is important that you recognize your part in the problems that arise and be willing to work on them.

Remember that biases can blind people to the point that they do not see the issues in their relationship. This is why developing self-

awareness can be challenging. However, as you gain more awareness of your partner's personality and your own, you will be able to identify your biases more easily. Once you take misunderstandings and misinterpretations out of the equation, you will be able to see positive changes in the relationship.

Self-awareness means being conscious of your own thoughts, how your mental state is at any given time, and how well you deal with your emotions, also known as emotional stability.

Let's take a closer look at all of the different aspects of self-awareness.

5.2 Thoughts and Emotions, which differences?

First things first. What are feelings and emotions? Many people use those two words interchangeably, but feelings and emotions are actually not the same thing.

Without getting too technical, we can say that emotions are responses to positive or negative triggers. Emotions are universal.

This means that everyone experiences the same emotions, regardless of their background, place of birth, education, etc.

Scientists can't seem to pin down an exact number of emotions—some claim there are only four while others count as many as 27.

The main four that they all agree on are happiness, sadness, fear, and anger.

On the other hand, feelings are a person's response to an emotion. Feelings differ from person to person as they're affected by personal beliefs, memories and experiences, hormones, and neurotransmitters.

The way we react—or "feel"—to a certain emotion may also change as our experiences shape and change us. At the same time, they may also help us realize things we may not have been aware of before.

For example, a person may realize they have feelings of love for someone once they see the other person showing romantic interest in someone else and react with feelings of jealousy.

Now that we got the basics down, let's move on.

5.3 Control your feelings

Feelings and emotions differ in another fundamental way.

Namely, we actually have control over our feelings to a certain extent. In fact, many people do try to manage their feelings to avoid being overwhelmed by them. The problem is that they go about it in potentially harmful ways, such as smothering, denying, or numbing feelings they deem to be negative. In such cases, the troubling feelings may subside momentarily.

Still, they will almost surely come back out in full force later on, which will only make the person feel even more discouraged, depressed, or anxious.

Another course of action people takes to control their feelings is overanalyzing. This approach is the polar opposite of the previous one, but it can be just as damaging.

The person becomes incapable of thinking about anything else but the troubling feelings as they try to find an answer or solution. When they find no clear solution, they can get sucked into an endless pattern of feeling anxious and depressed, not only because of the original, negative feeling but also because they have no way to fix it. In other words, they feel bad about feeling bad.

Yet other people can find a sort of happy medium when it comes to managing their emotions. For instance, they may suppress their feelings while they're at work, but allow themselves the freedom to express them when they're at home or with someone who loves and understands them. Because the person feels safe, they don't feel the need to keep their guard up, smother their feelings, or overthink why they feel the way they do. This course of action is closer to the merciful mindfulness and self-

awareness we've been talking about. Being aware of our feelings and emotions and giving ourselves permission to feel them, we can ride the waves of our changing feelings rather than drowning in them.

Let's look at the rather extreme example of the loss of a spouse.

The way many people handle grief is to avoid the feelings of loss and misery. They may throw themselves into their work, start new home-improvement projects, take up a new hobby, anything to avoid feeling grief. They are physically and mentally incapable of facing this torrent of negative emotions, they become more and more numb to their feelings, and ultimately stop interacting with other people in a profound manner.

Conversely, somebody who more willing to face their distress will, in time, be able to acknowledge and accept their troubling feelings.

This is the path to healing from a loss that may seem insurmountable at the time.

We're not saying any of this is easy. Far from it.

Dealing with painful feelings is very, very difficult. It takes a lot of courage, patience, and, you guessed it, self-love. You have to permit yourself to feel

whatever it is you're feeling. Any feeling you have is valid, because it comes as a direct result of your experiences. Denying your feelings, trying to suppress them, or forcing yourself to come up with a solution to deal with them will only result in even more heartache.

5.3 Identify your feelings

We're going to start this section with an example.

Gerry has been feeling very unhappy with his marriage. He decides to talk to his friend,

Gertrude, about it. He's very agitated—he's crying, talking very fast, alternating between rage and sadness.

Gerry tells Gertrude that he can't confide in his spouse anymore. He feels his partner has been increasingly distant and may even be cheating on him. He talks about all the fights they've had and how they seem to be getting worse. Gerry is confused and doesn't know what to do anymore.

Gertrude listens patiently to Gerry and then tells him to take a deep breath.

Once Gerry has calmed down, his friend suggests that he try to figure out how he feels about the situation so that he can calmly and efficiently find a solution. After some introspection, Gerry

discovers that he feels angry, sad, disappointed, scared, insecure,

and betrayed.

Giving your feelings the right name is the best way to distinguish them, which, in turn, helps you not to be overwhelmed by them. It's always a good idea to take a step away from your problems and give yourself some time to really understand your feelings.

Even if it's only for a couple of minutes, taking this pause can really help you in the process of understanding and eventually healing from painful situations.

In fact, let's give that a try right now. What are you feeling at this very moment? Take all the time you need to identify, separate, and name each of your current feelings.

Notice how you have gone from being a passive receptacle for your feelings, to actively distinguishing and naming each one. Being able to do this is instrumental in the process of giving yourself permission to experience your feelings and not being overwhelmed by them. Try to practice this technique as often as you can. An ideal approach is to practice when your feelings aren't too strong or negative.

Positive and "soft" feelings have a lower probability of overwhelming you.

For instance, you can do this exercise first thing in the morning,

as you shower, or right before bed. The main goal is for you to discover how you experience your feelings by directing your attention to them, identifying, and intentionally observing them. The more you practice this technique, the easier it will be to apply to more serious feelings.

Furthermore, as you get better at it, you will be able to gain a more objective perspective of your problems and thus find better solutions for them.

Thoughts can be very powerful triggers for feelings, whether positive or negative. We have said this before, but thoughts like "my partner doesn't really love me. They just stay with me out of obligation/pity/boredom/etc.," can trigger feelings of depression, anxiety, fear, and self-loathing.

Whether we realize it or not, there is a constant torrent of thoughts running through the background of our minds. Becoming aware of these thoughts can be very useful in distinguishing and, later, managing our feelings. If we learn to eliminate self-deprecating thoughts such as the one above, we can fundamentally change our relationship's dynamic.

Now that you have identified and named your current feelings, let's take things one step further.

Find a quiet place where you won't be interrupted. Close your eyes and take a couple of deep breaths.

Do a full-body scan, from your head to your toes, and identify any sensations in your body.

Is there pain anywhere? Do you feel any muscle strain? How is your breathing? Is it easy or labored? Is your heart rate normal or accelerated?

Now, pick one of the feelings you have already identified and named.

Focus all your attention on it and try to what effects it has on your body.

What sensations do you feel now? If it's a positive feeling, do you feel calmer?

Maybe your breathing and your heart rate have slowed down.

On the other hand, if it's a negative feeling, perhaps you feel pain somewhere in your body, like your stomach.

Maybe you're breathing faster or are holding your breath altogether.

Try doing this activity whenever you experience any strong feelings, positive or negative. You will gradually start to learn what sensations accompany any given feeling, which will be very helpful for your

process of self-awareness. If you know beforehand how you usually react to, say, frustration, you will be able to reign in your feelings and handle them calmly rather than blowing up at your partner.

Additionally, if you make it a habit to slow down and give yourself some time to explore your emotions and sensations, over time, you will start to feel lighter, more joyful, and maybe even diminish aches and pains.

Mentalization is another aspect of mindful awareness.

Essentially, mentalization is the process of understanding what's going on in our minds, as well as other people's. We are able to understand other people's and our own behavior based on our state of mind, feelings, needs, desires, etc.

In practical terms, this allows us to discover rational explanations behind our actions, and other people's. Individuals who practice mentalization can completely alter their perception of their relationships.

It can also provide us with a higher level of empathy for ourselves and other people's problems.

Not many people practice, or even know about, mentalization,

though. Therefore, while they may have some superficial idea of why others do and feel the way they do, it is by no means a profound understanding.

The same goes for their own actions and feelings. They perceive themselves as defective for feeling the way they do, to the point that they feel undeserving of empathy. They also have a tendency to blame themselves for all the issues in their relationship.

Here's an example. Maxwell, a man with an anxious attachment style, is about to go on a first date with someone he met recently. The evening is pleasant enough, and, at the end of the night, Maxwell asks his date if they would like to go out again soon. Maxwell's date politely declines.

Maxwell doesn't respond very well do this. He is left feelingmiserable about the whole thing, trying to figure out what he did to mess it up. This rejection reinforces his belief that there's something wrong with him; that he doesn't deserve love.

But what if Maxwell was more self-aware and practiced mentalization? Sure, the rejection might still hurt a bit. No one, no matter how self-aware, enjoys rejection, after all. However, the reaction wouldn't be so extreme.

He would easily understand that not everyone clicks and that being rejected by one person doesn't make him unlovable or unworthy. He may even remember times when he refused someone because the other person just wasn't compatible with him. Maxwell will then be able to get over this incident, with no hard feelings for the other person, and no feelings of self-loathing.

There is something important you need to keep in mind, though.

Practicing mentalization doesn't mean that difficult situations will never again bring you pain. It isn't uncommon for people to think something along the lines of, "I know I'm scared of being rejected because my dad left when I was a kid. But it happened so long ago, I should have gotten over it by now."

The truth is that some events will bring us pain, no matter how self-aware we are. There's no way around that. However, learning how to react with self-compassion can help ease that pain.

Mentalization may sound like a complicated thing to do, and

sometimes it can be. But if you start with baby steps, like identifying and naming your feelings and discovering the sensations they trigger on your body, you will soon get to a point where you'll have a deep understanding of your own state of mind and behaviors.

Understanding and having empathy for other people will naturally follow.

We will talk about some more activities to improve your mentalization technique in the following chapter.

5.4 Self-Compassion

We have discussed at length how self-awareness can help you have a healthier and happier relationship. But if you've been paying attention, you'll see that there's one more factor that is absolutely imperative for self-awareness to work. That factor is self-compassion.

People don't usually just react to a situation, experience feelings, understand them, and move on.

We also tend to judge ourselves for having those feelings. We have thoughts like, "I shouldn't be feeling this way," or "I'm pathetic for reacting this way."

This mindset is terribly toxic and detrimental to our mental health. That's why it is so important to always practice self-compassion along with self-awareness.

An interesting thing to point out is that people often display more

empathy and compassion for other people than for themselves.

When someone we love is suffering, we go out of our way to try to

make them feel better. We dish out our best advice and give them all our love and support.

It's high time we started doing the same thing for ourselves.

The best way to go about practicing self-compassion is to start by being kind to yourself. This means treating yourself with love and support when you feel pain, disappointment, or inadequacy.

Instead of condemning and judging yourself for feeling this way, you have to accept that this is just how you feel, and there is nothing wrong with it.

Many people will argue that self-compassion will only cause people to become complacent, self-satisfied, or egotistical.

They may believe that being kind to yourself means letting yourself off the hook for everything you do. This couldn't be further from the truth.

Genuine self-compassion isn't meant for us to forego the consequences of our actions. People who practice compassion, for themselves and other people, can accomplish truly wonderful and humane work, whether on a large scale—like Nelson Mandela or Martin Luther King Jr.—or in their social circle.

And the truth is, we can't be genuinely compassionate for other people until we learn to be compassionate for ourselves first.

This means acknowledging that all people feel similar emotions, such as pain and disappointment, and have similar experiences like shortcomings and flaws.

When we genuinely understand that every person on the planet feels the same things we do, we begin to feel less detached and alone. We become capable of understanding that all our problems are

simply part of being human and that these challenges don't imply that there's something wrong with them.

Therefore, being more humane will help us form stronger connections with other people, including our significant other.

5.5 Practice mindfulness

Mindfulness is a mental state in which we are aware of the present moment while acknowledging and accepting our thoughts and

emotions without judgment.

When you practice mindfulness during confrontations with other people, there won't be any need to deny, smother, or overstate your

feelings.

You will have a clear and objective perspective of both your and your partner's point of view, which will lead to a higher level of compassion. You will also be able to find solutions to your problems more effectively.

For example, people who are sensitive to the feeling of being rejected might lose their temper if they perceive their partner is being neglectful. They might lash out or become distant. In both cases, they end up driving their partner away, which is the exact opposite of what they genuinely want and need.

We've talked about people who try to smother or deny their feelings instead of mindfully acknowledging them. When they do this, those feelings frequently return with considerably more force.

Paradoxically, if the people who do this instead tried to be more

aware of their feelings, they would not feel as overwhelmed by them. Even in the middle of a conflict, they would be able to react in ways that are conducive to solving the problem.

These three components of self-compassion—self-kindness, humanity, and mindfulness—are crucial in developing self-love.

When we become more nurturing of ourselves, we will, in turn, become more nurturing for the people around us, including out significant other.

Additionally, we will be able to handle any conflict we have with them in a healthy way that leads to a happy and long-lasting relationship.

5.6 Self-Compassion and his Power

As we mentioned before, people who practice self-compassion

experience times of trouble and pain, just everyone else. They also need understanding, help, love, and support from others.

The main difference is that they tend to be considerably more

tolerating of themselves. Self-compassionate people are better at maintaining stable relationships and have a more objective perspective when they make mistakes or are having a difficult time.

Cultivating self-compassion takes a lot of work, but this shouldn't discourage you. Through mindfulness, you will gradually be able to develop it and have a more joyous relationship with yourself and others as a result.

Whether you're currently in a relationship or not, you can still begin to cultivate empathy toward yourself. To explain how this works, let's talk about Jane.

She is a forty-five-year-old woman who wants to get married. She recently met Oliver and was instantly besotted with him. They soon start a relationship.

Jane, who is looking for something serious, makes the decision to give herself fully to the relationship. She opens up to Oliver about her feelings, confident that he will love her no matter what.

Sometimes she's scared that he'll reject her, but she is able to fight those feelings and be open and honest with him.

Even so, as the relationship progresses, she starts to feel that

something's not quite right in their relationship (awareness of feelings). She has started to think things like, "it's not much fun when we spend time together," or "he can be a little irritating at times" (awareness of thoughts). However, she has also realized that she misses him when they spend a lot of time apart (awareness of feelings and thoughts).

Jane decides to do some serious introspection to figure out why she has such contradictory feelings without judging herself because of it.

With the assistance of mentalization, she is able to understand that the problem isn't that she doesn't love Oliver. The root of the issue is that she has subconsciously been looking for reasons not to commit more fully to him for fear of being rejected.

Armed with this knowledge, she can see her feelings and behaviors are justifiable and human (self-compassion).

Instead of breaking up with Oliver, Jane has another alternative—to confront her fear of rejection. After a lot of help and support from her friends, she is finally ready to talk to Oliver about the problems she's been having. Oliver, who also practices self-awareness, self-compassion, and mentalization, understands Jane's feelings and accepts her nonetheless.

Without awareness of thoughts and feelings, mentalization, and self-

compassion, Jane's story probably wouldn't have had such a happy ending. She may have concluded that there was no real connection between her and Oliver and broken up with him.

Or, even worse, they would have gotten married without ever addressing these feelings. This may have resulted in Jane feeling increasingly distant from Oliver. As a result, Oliver would have felt unloved and underappreciated in their marriage.

To sum up, self-compassion and self-awareness are crucial techniques to practice if you want to have a successful relationship. They can help you understand your conflicts and approach them

mindfully and humanely, allowing you to have the relationship you deserve finally.

Chapter 6: Develop Self-Awareness

As we have said before, developing self-awareness is no easy task. People are so scared of change that they stick to their old behavior patterns and attachment styles even though they bring nothing but pain and loneliness.

Be aware that you may feel the urge to skip one or more of the following exercises. This is perfectly normal. This resistance can be due to any number of factors, but more often than not, it may be because it's related to some aspect of yourself that you're in denial about or that you intensely dislike.

Permit yourself to feel this opposition, but be ready to work through it.

It might be uncomfortable, but we urge you to power through the feelings of discomfort. This is precisely what you need to do on the most.

Start by opening yourself up to the possibility of change. From that point, you will start to develop awareness of your thoughts and feelings gradually. You will also become more mindful and compassionate about these feelings and improve your mentalization technique. The following sections will provide you with different ways to approach each of these areas of self-awareness.

Whether you're still looking for a relationship or already in one, you can also use these techniques to genuinely try to get to know and understand your partner better.

6.1 Vulnerability

If you want to have a stable and prosperous romantic relationship, you need to be ready to open up to your partner. Letting ourselves be vulnerable can be scary, but it's one of the most important things you can do if you want your relationship to succeed. Understanding this will also help you see past your biases and behaviors that have contributed to unsuccessful past relationships.

For example, Manuela is a woman who is terribly scared of rejection.

When she was in a relationship with someone she truly loved, all Manuela could do to protect herself from the possibility of rejection was to tell herself that she didn't really love her partner that much.

"Even if my partner leaves me, I'll be fine. I don't really love my partner that much, so I'm sure I'll be able to find someone better eventually."

This mindset only caused a significant rift between Manuela and her partner, which is precisely what Manuela feared the most.

Had Manuela been aware of her own feelings of love for her partner and fear of rejection, she might have been more open to talking about her issues. In that case, she would have at least had a fighting chance to save her relationship.

By confronting your inner conflicts, you will likewise be facing the fear that you are undeserving of love and the destructive thoughts

that your partner doesn't care about you. You will start to recognize signs of self-sabotage and eventually eliminate those tendencies from your life.

Remember to take your time and work at your own pace! This isn't a race, and you don't get points for pushing yourself to emotional exhaustion. Some great ways to pace yourself so you're not overwhelmed:

Pick your battles. If you're only just starting to practice self-awareness, don't feel bad if you sometimes forget. The habit of being mindful is one that develops over time

Take a time-out. If you feel that you're being overwhelmed by your emotions, go somewhere quiet for a few minutes and take some deep breaths. Come back to the exercise once you've calmed down and feel ready to do so

Keep a journal of your progress. Write down the emotions you identified and named that day and how they affected you.

Keep a record of what you have discovered about yourself through mentalization.

Share what you're doing to someone you trust. Talk to a friend or family member, or even your romantic partner, about your journey to self-awareness.

Having someone to share your victories and struggles with can really make this a whole lot easier.

And who knows? You may even inspire them to do the same!

It is also crucial not to take extreme measures at the beginning of your mindful practice. For example, suppose that you realize that your partner is often dismissive of your feelings. This doesn't mean that you should end the relationship right then and there.

This is where you can use mentalization to, first, understand why your partner may be acting this way, and second, start a conversation with them about it.

Confronting the challenge of being vulnerable is something you'll have to do more than once from here on out, but you must stay determined and brave. Soon you will realize that being true to yourself only means healthier and happier connections with other people.

6.2 Your Feelings

Many people find it difficult to recognize their own feelings. If you're one of those people, it might be because you've become alienated from them.

Or maybe you just don't know how to find the words to express them.

Whatever the reason, the first step you have to take is to attach general descriptions to your feelings. For example, "I feel upset" or "I feel irritated."

If you have an anxiety disorder or depression, you will likely notice that your feelings can be very extreme and often strike in what seems like a huge mass of unidentifiable emotions.

However, identifying and naming each of your feelings can have a grounding effect, potentially helping you get through difficult moments. We've already talked about how to identify your feelings, but we'll go over that exercise step by step one more time.

Find a quiet place where you won't be disturbed Close your eyes and take five deep breaths.

Pick out a single core emotion: happiness, sadness, fear, or anger

If you find one these emotions in yourself, identify it and focus on it Identify the feelings accompanying your chosen emotion.

For example, if you're experiencing anger, do you feel irritated?

Maybe you feel annoyed, jealous, envious, disappointed, etc.

Name these feelings and write them down in a notebook as you discover them

Feel free to write down as many as you want, but remember: don't judge yourself

If you feel up to up, try repeating this exercise with other core sensations you may be experiencing at the moment

As you work through this exercise, it's important that you build up the capacity to open up to your feelings and close yourself off to them to a certain extent.

For instance, say you were going through some feelings of anxiety.

So you sat down to identify and name your feelings and have

discovered that you're currently experiencing fear of rejection.

The deeper you look into this feeling, the more likely the possibility that it will become even more intense. This is normal, and it's a big reason

why you should only start this practice in a safe environment.

Additionally, once you have identified your fear, you might even have the feeling something "clicking." In other words, knowing that you're experiencing fear of rejection feels "right." This is because your fear is a real and valid experience that you're going through at that moment.

However, diving so deep into this feeling may not be something you're ready for just yet. In that case, after you have acknowledged and allowed yourself to feel your fear, it might become necessary to pull out of it to avoid becoming overwhelmed. When this happens, take some more deep breaths, as many as you need to calm down.

If possible, try to direct your attention to something you find pleasant immediately: read a book, make some tea, watch a movie, listen to some music. Anything goes as long as it makes you happy.

6.3 Prepare yourself to endure and persevere through difficult emotions.

Your body language and behavior are a treasure trove of hidden clues for what you're truly feeling. If you want to get to know your inner self and identify your feelings more accurately, you should be tapping into these resources as often as possible.

One of the best ways to do so is by talking about your feelings with other people. Ask a close friend, family member, or significant other to listen to you without judgment. You can even ask them to give you some feedback on how they perceive your body language and behavior as you talk. Do you seem closed off and uncomfortable? Maybe you're not being very open about the true extent of your feelings. Do they see your body language as open and relaxed? You're on the right track to genuine self-awareness.

As you open up to mindfulness, it is fundamental that you be prepared to endure and persevere through difficult emotions. Keeping an open and flexible mindset will empower you through this process and help you manage your feelings.

You can increase your resilience to unsettling feelings by surrendering yourself to them through care and reflection, which we'll discuss further in Chapter 8.

You can likewise do it by moving toward your feelings with interest.

Another critical factor for developing perseverance is to be genuinely interested and curious about your feelings and behavior patterns.

This curiosity will be a great tool in discovering your most hidden feelings, despite any resistance you may feel. It stands to reason that the more interested you are in yourself and your emotions, the more thoroughly you will investigate them to discover their effect on your life.

6.3 Use Your Thoughts to make friends

As you start to get a better understanding of your feelings, you will also learn how to control them and, eventually, how to make them your allies. Moreover, you will discover the value your emotions bring to your life. For example, you may start to value your loneliness

since because it inspires you to meet new people.

Knowing and accepting your feelings also helps you exercise self-restraint.

You won't feel the need to blow up at people whenever something irritates you.

Figuring out how your own feelings and making peace with them can be a drawn-out or undertaking, but well worth the effort.

6.4 Change Your Thoughts immediately

Although we've talked about the difference between thoughts and feelings, the truth is that the distinction between the two isn't that significant.

Our perspective on any given circumstance frequently influences our feelings. For example, you may feel profoundly miserable when you think about how you believe someone you care about doesn't like you and finds you boring. In this situation, you may say things like, "I feel terrible," or "I'm a failure," or "this sucks."

But these words are reflections of your thoughts, not actual feelings. Consequently, as you try to identify your feelings, you notice that they are impacted by or intermixed with your thoughts.

As we mentioned in the previous chapter, your thoughts directly impact you on many levels. So if negative thoughts have the power to make you feel bad, it's reasonable to say that you can substitute them with more positive and beneficial ones to feel better.

For example, say you're prone to thinking along the lines of, "Ihaven't had a romantic relationship in a long time. I'm such a failure." Whenever you catch yourself thinking that, immediately try to replace that with a more neutral or positive message: "I haven't met anyone I'm compatible with yet, but it will happen eventually."

If you open yourself to genuinely accept this new thought, you will notice how your feelings will gradually become more positive.

Remember to be patient with yourself. This is a long and challenging process. You're fundamentally altering your self-perceptions and frame of mind, after all. Something you have lived with for your entire life. So it will take some considerable effort to build up a new perspective and behavior pattern.

The most important thing is that you become progressively mindful of your self-reflections and how they influence you.

By doing this, you are laying down the groundwork required to understand your thoughts and feelings about yourself and your relationship.

This will enhance your awareness of how your emotions work and how you relate and react to them.

Your negative thoughts—about yourself or your partner's shortcomings—only serve to fuel your anxiety.

To really change your negative thoughts, and potentially decrease their impact on you, try doing the following exercise.

Grab a notebook and pen and make a table with the following sections:

Date

Event.

Try to write down as many details as you can about what happened. Don't go into your thoughts and feelings yet, only describe the factual circumstances.

Attachment-Related Anxious Thoughts. This is where you jot down all the negative thoughts that when through your mind during the event described above.

These thoughts can be about both yourself and your partner if they were involved.

Effects of Thoughts on Feelings and Behaviors. Remember the exercise to identify your feelings? Do it again now and write down what feelings this situation triggered for you.

Also write down how your behavior changed from before the incident occurred, to while it was ongoing, to after it was finished.

Disconfirming Evidence. This part can be tricky. What we're looking for here is evidence that your thoughts and feelings are biased and not entirely based on the truth.

Suppose the event was a fight between you and your partner. Under such circumstances, your anger or sadness could be causing you to see yourself or your significant other under a negative light.

Bring to mind the times when you were happy with your relationship and see if you can find any actions you or your partner took that disprove the negative image you have now.

Suppose the disconfirming evidence instills genuine uncertainty, and you become able to acknowledge the negative impacts of your reasoning.

In that case, you can start to develop a progressively positive viewpoint as you keep exploring your feelings. Keeping the disconfirming proof in mind when you feel uneasy about this event will really help you get past it. Make up your mind to focus on the more positive and practical techniques of approaching any future events similar to this one.

For example, when you feel restless about your partner being distant, notice that they do that when they're busy.

Try to remember all the times they messaged you or called you out the blue to see how you were.

On the other hand, if there isn't any uncertainty about your negative view of yourself, then this might be a part of your behavior that you should work on.

If the negative thought you were unable to disprove is about your partner, this might be an ideal opportunity to address this issue with them.

As you do this, though, always remember to practice compassion, both for yourself and for your partner.

Mentalization is another way you can increase the intimacy in your relationship since it basically gives you a window into your partner's reality. When you strive for a deeper understanding of your

significant other, you will truly see the world through their eyes, including their feelings and thoughts.

Keep in mind that you don't necessarily have to agree with your partner's mindset and behavior pattern.

You also don't need a perfectly detailed first-person perspective on your partner's everyday life. Simply having an idea of how they feel and, most importantly, why, will help you feel closer to them.

Mindfulness requires tolerance. You have to be open to replacing your old perception of yourself and your partner with a new, more accurate awareness of your thoughts, emotions, and actions.

Whenever you mind yourself struggling, remember to do the activities we have shown you in this and previous chapters, talk with your partner or confide in your loved ones.

Most importantly, continue developing better approaches to interact with yourself and with the people close to you.

Chapter 7: Communication is the key for an Happy Relationship

Good communication skills are crucial if you want to have successful relationships with other people.

Ensuring that you have an open communication with your partner will help you build a long-lasting and happy relationship.

By contrast, people with poor communication skills are much more likely to have unresolved fights and unhealthy relationships.

Not being able to communicate properly will also cause you to become more defensive when it comes to your partner.

You might unintentionally focus on winning an argument rather than solving your issues.

The way you were raised and your current beliefs play an essential role in determining how you communicate with others.

Your past experiences provide you with the parameters that determine how you interact with your partner.

Still, these experiences are long gone and not a real part of your current life. Clinging to unhealthy old viewpoints will only cause more problems for you and your partner in the long run. It's time to adopt new communication methods and snub the old practices and communication styles that you might have developed over the years.

In this chapter, we will cover the skills required to improve your communication with your partner.

7.1 Self-Disclosure

Most of us have spent our lives hiding our insecurities and vulnerabilities from other people. We get scared when we think about sharing or revealing a secret about ourselves. This triggers feelings of guilt, shame, and fear. When you share the vulnerabilities with a stranger or someone you don't know very well, this can potentially lead to more insecurities. Without meaning to, the other person can challenge our core beliefs, which can trigger anxiety or depression.

This isn't meant to discourage you from being vulnerable and showing other people your most genuine self. What you want to do is find a balance between sharing and withholding information. Sharing your vulnerability with your closest friends or your partner can be liberating, and it's a great way to strengthen your bond.

Do you feel unloved in your relationship? Do you hide your true self and wish you could open up more with your partner? Do you feel happy and safe in your relationship, or do you feel that love is decreasing? Will opening up to your partner help you heal the relationship and reduce anxiety? All these thoughts will challenge your core beliefs and may be difficult for you to fully understand at first. But facing them head-on is the only way forward, away from toxic viewpoints and behavior patterns.

7.2 Rewards of Self-Disclosure Listening Skills

Self-disclosure can lead to long-lasting relationships, reduced anxiety, and elimination of the feeling of abandonment. Some of the many benefits of self-disclosure are listed below.

More energy - Hiding your true self and keeping up appearances can be exhausting. It's the burden you have to bear when you choose to hide your true self from the world. You won't be able to feel the joy of having a deep and genuine conversation with someone else, since you will be in constant fear of sharing any information about yourself that you want to keep hidden.

Taking off your masks will free up an immense amount of energy that you can invest in improving your relationship with yourself and your partner.

Eliminate feelings of guilt - Chronic feelings of guilt can change a person's entire life. But keeping all the parts of yourself that you feel ashamed of hidden is impossible to sustain. Remember that imperfections are a part of life, and when you start hiding things from the people you love, you will begin the ensuing of shame and guilt can take over your whole life.

Improve communication - When you open up to your partner, chances are you will inspire them to do the same. This will naturally lead to better communication between you. Make an effort to share your true self with your partner. You will find yourself sharing the most intimate details about your life and living happily together in no time.

More intimate relationships - Disclosing personal information and sharing your feelings will help you form closer bonds with the people you love. This will lead to more meaningful interactions with those around you. Surely a welcome change from the unsatisfying and shallow relationship you might have had in the past.

Increased self-knowledge - We're all pretty well-aware of all the secrets we keep. So you might be wondering how sharing them with your partner can increase knowledge about yourself.

The truth is, when you don't share your feelings with anyone, you tend to make assumptions that have no real basis in facts.

Moreover, going over and over your secrets in your mind will never provide you with any real closure.

Sharing this information with your partner will give you a new and fresh perspective, and you will be eager to find out even more information that can help you solve these issues.

7.3 Pseudo-Listening vs. Real Listening

Developing your listening skills is probably the most crucial step to bridge the communication gap between you and your partner. When someone feels truly heard, they tend to feel empowered, loved, supported, and understood. We live in a busy world where people rarely have time to sit down and reflect on their own feelings, let alone listen to someone else's.

This is why it is imperative to develop your listening skills if you want your partner to feel loved and cared for.

But before we talk about something called "active listening", which is our goal, we need to show you the difference between really listening and pseudo-listening.

7.4 Listening Blocks

Pseudo-listening is a concept that we should all be aware of. As you may have guessed, pseudo-listening is only half-listening to what the other person is saying, not really paying much attention. One sign of pseudo-listening is when you start thinking about how to reply to what the other person is saying before they're done talking.

Another is when you engage in other activities, such as looking at your phone, when someone is talking. This can lead to many issues since people who have this habit have trouble keeping successful relationships. They're unable to fully process the information that other people share with them, which can be harmful to the relationship.

Not feeling heard might also trigger feelings of anxiety in someone with Fearful or Preoccupied Attachment styles.

You need to make it a habit to listen, really listen to what other people say.

Numerous things can hinder your capacity to remain focused on what the other person is trying to say to you. The vast majority of us have been in an icebreaker type of situation in class, at a retreat, or a meeting where everybody is required to stand up and say something about themselves.

If you've even been in that situation yourself, you probably remember that your attention was mostly focused on what you were going to say about yourself than what other people were saying. Maybe you practiced your speech in your mind over and over to avoid making mistakes, or we just too anxious about speaking publicly. Some people just have a short attention span and need to be doing many things at once.

Whatever the cause, listening blocks can only have a damaging effect on your relationship.

7.5 Active Listening

If you feel that your communication skills require some work and want to improve your relationships, you need to introduce active listening to your daily routine. Knowing about pseudo-listening and listening blocks is a good first step, but good communication requires additional work.

When you start to truly listen to other people, you will be able to respond more insightfully, in a way that makes them feel you dully support them.

Everything from your words, actions, and body language will show that you are really paying attention.

Next, we will talk about three techniques you can use to focus your attention on the other person and make them feel heard without judgment.

7.6 Paraphrasing

Paraphrasing is expressing the meaning of what someone else has said using different words. A practical example might help to make the concept clearer.

Person A: I don't think my partner cares about me anymore. They never reply to my messages or calls anymore.

Person B: So you feel neglected because your partner isn't talking to you as often as they used to?

In paraphrasing, you use your own words to help you focus on what the other person is saying and to show that you understand the meaning they're trying to convey.

Everyone has different core beliefs and, therefore, different ways to communicate. By using paraphrasing, you will be able to have more

meaningful conversations because you're adapting the other person's words to your core beliefs using your own words.

This can potentially eliminate any cognitive distortions and false assumptions.

7.7 Clarifying

Consider clarifying as an addition to paraphrasing. In this step, you will ask questions until you understand what the other person is trying to communicate. Look at the example above once more. Notice how Person B not only paraphrased Person A's statement but also turned it into a question? This is the idea behind clarification.

With this process, you will be able to gather more information and know what message the other person is trying to convey. This will also send a positive message to the speaker: they will know that you are actively participating in the conversation.

7.8 Feedback

The third and final step is providing feedback. After you fully absorb and comprehend the information presented to you, it's time to share your thoughts. Once you have assimilated their words, you offer a message back, communicating that you have listened to the speaker and want to engage in a meaningful dialogue.

The key to providing meaningful feedback is to offer a message free of judgment. When the speaker receives positive feedback from you, they know that you understand their side of the story and will feel empowered. This will also lead to less anxiety in the relationship.

There are three basic rules you should follow when giving feedback. The feedback should be honest (even if it's painful), it should be immediate, and it should have a supportive tone.

One last thing to keep in mind is that sometimes people will share their problems with others just to get it out of their chest and may not be looking for advice or feedback. Always make sure you ask the speaker if they want feedback before you provide it.

7.9 Expressing Your Needs Validation

Do you remember the last time you told someone that you needed them? Expressing your needs may seem like an easy thing to do, but it can be very difficult. Many people just aren't used to asking for attention or expressing their needs. Yet others may think they don't actually need anything from other people.

The main problem people face is that we have become more alienated from the concept of expressing our needs. Many people have probably gone years without it. We might get the urge to communicate our needs to our friends, family members, or romantic partner, but we often smother and ignore it. This is most likely because we fear rejection, which could increase the problems in the relationship.

However, you should keep in mind that if you've been rejected before or have faced problems after expressing your needs, it does not mean that it will happen to you again.

If you can overcome your fears and open up to your partner, the result may just be that they acknowledge and accept your needs.

People aren't mind readers. You significant other can't know what you want if you don't speak up. So if you choose to express your needs to them, they will have a better understanding of how to make you happy.

With this simple change, you will be able to eliminate the stress and anxiety from your relationship and live more happily with your partner.

Remember that this is a two-way street, too. As you open up to your partner about your needs, they will feel comfortable and safe enough to do the same.

If you're still worried about expressing your needs, there are a few ways you can make this concept less intimidating.

Try unpackaging your needs. This means that you analyze each one, so know how much you're asking for and start with needs that seem less demanding. Gradually, you'll be able to tackle your "bigger" needs with less anxiety.

If you find that your needs clash with your partner's core beliefs, try to understand their perspective. In a stable relationship, you will be able to work something out and find common ground where both of your needs will be accepted and met. Remember that mentalization is a great tool for this.

You might be familiar with this term and how important it is to develop a healthy relationship. In this section, we will tell you how verbal and nonverbal validation plays a role in forming a good relationship.

Validation is the process in which you express to the person you're talking to that you're listening to them. It doesn't mean that you agree or disagree with their thoughts.

Validation only means that you understand why they feel the way they do and accept it and their core beliefs.

The process of verification we talked about earlier is a great way to offer validation to the speaker. This is because verification opens a dialogue between you and the other person.

If your partner expresses their feelings and you respond with acknowledgment and acceptance and do not judge them, this will let them know that you care about their thoughts and feelings. As a result, they will confide in you more and more.

Validation also helps to increase self-disclosure. Again, verification comes in handy. When someone asks you more questions about your thoughts, feelings, and experiences, you will likely feel more confident about sharing that information.

When people don't receive validation during their early years, they tend to become more closed-off to their own feelings and needs. This will cause feelings of dissatisfaction, disappointment, loneliness, hopelessness, etc., once they become adults.

Experiencing empathy, or relating to other people's emotions, can be a very powerful experience.

As we mentioned earlier, everyone has their own set of core beliefs that are a direct result of their past experiences.

The vast majority of us have experienced pain at one time or another, and we've all been through varying degrees of hardship. Therefore, it would help our interactions with other people if we made an effort to keep in mind that everyone is fighting their own internal battles. Think about it as our shared human factor.

It's also true that we all struggle and deal with our problems in different ways. Even someone who appears to be outwardly fine could be grappling with their personal issues.

Additionally, we may disagree with how another person manages their pain. But the truth is that we're all doing our best to heal. You don't need to agree with someone in order to understand what it's like to be in pain.

Empathy means simply that. Understanding that the other person is suffering and accepting that the way they feel is valid, without passing judgment.

7.10 Empathy and Apologize

As we practice self-awareness and empathy, we will quickly realize when our words or actions hurt someone. What we should do when that Apologizing for our mistakes, especially if they bring other people pain, is one of the most powerful tools to bring peace to someone's life. You will be able to connect to the other person's experiences and core beliefs.

Sadly, many people never learned how to apologize. This could be due to a number of reasons. Maybe the person's parents never apologized to anyone when they did something wrong. Or perhaps they instilled in their children the belief that apologizing was a sign of weakness. Apologizing means accepting our mistakes and shortcomings, after all, so many people fear that others will see them as defective and they will lose face.

Not knowing when to apologize can lead to problems in your personal and professional life, though. At a basic level, you won't be able to relate to another person's pain. You won't know how to control your words and actions to avoid hurting others.

The phrasing is extremely important when you apologize to another person. You need to make it clear to them that you've realized your mistake and genuinely want to make amends.

Your tone and actions should reflect that you know that the other person is hurt, and you feel sorry for having caused that pain. The last thing you want to do is apologize with insincere words. Your apology should come from the heart.

You also shouldn't hesitate when you have to apologize to the people you love, including your partner. A well-timed apology will only help to bring you closer together.

If you're not very good at apologizing yet, don't worry.

Like everything else, learning how to apologize is a process, and it may take some time until you develop this skill.

It takes some practice, but with a little effort, your relationships will be even healthier and happier.

In this chapter, we introduced the communication skills that you need to formulate long-lasting loving relationships. All these skills are vital, and with some effort, you will be able to master them all in no time.

Keep in mind that these skills are not just meant to be used with your romantic partner.

Good communication can also enhance your professional and family life. You should always engage in meaningful dialogue when you feel confused about your partner's beliefs, thoughts, and emotions.

Chapter 8: Why Cultivate the Self-Compassion it's so important

Being deliberately mindful of your perceptions about yourself and your partner isn't easy. The distress it can potentially cause can trigger you to look for consolation by abandoning your developing mindfulness and going back to your old inclinations. So to help keep your developing mindfulness on a progressively positive course, you will need to cultivate self-compassion alongside it.

As mentioned before, self-compassion will make you increasingly better disposed to see yourself and your partner in a sensible yet positive light.

For instance, it can help you eliminate the propensity to see yourself as unlovable, regardless of whether your partner decides to end the relationship at some point. If this happens, you will know that it wasn't because you're inherently unlovable or flawed.

The more you acknowledge and accept the positive aspects of yourself, the better prepared you will be to handle moments of adversity. Think of your positive qualities as tools you can bring out of your toolbelt whenever you need to solve a problem.

Self-compassion will also help you to open up to other people without fear of rejection. Other people's opinions of you will no longer determine your sense of self-worth.

Developing this vital aspect of self-love also means that you will naturally search for healthier and more nurturing relationships.

You will also be more receptive to the positive moments of your interactions with other people, rather than focusing on the bad ones.

For example, let's consider Nikola. Her Dismissing Attachment style made it very difficult for her to open up to other people or accept affection.

She became shut-off increasingly from the world, preferring instead to remain alone at home.

Her feelings of loneliness became overpowering, though, and she knew she had to make a change.

She began cultivating self-compassion. She gradually started to accept the fact that, while she was as flawed as any other human on this planet, she was still deserving of love and companionship.

She started by taking art classes at the local college, where she met many new people, including Rosie, who gave the impression of being as nervous about meeting other people as Nikola herself.

By practicing mentalization and empathy, Nikola could easily relate to Rosie's apprehension and was able to reach out and comfort the other woman. This something Nikola would never have been able to do without practicing self-compassion first.

If you have ever been in a situation similar to Nikola's, you know how painful it is to feel separated from other people, believing you don't matter to anyone.

We're meant to have a human connection in order to thrive. When we have meaningful relationships, we feel needed and cared for, making it easier to be at peace with ourselves.

The following activities provide a practical way to go about cultivating self-compassion.

8.1 Why you have to practice Generosity

An excellent first step to cultivate compassion and empathy is to practice generosity towards yourself and others.

Hold the door open for other people, compliment a coworker's outfit, call a friend just to see how they're doing, offer your neighbor help if you see them struggling with something, do volunteer work for a cause you care about. When we perform acts of kindness from the heart, it can not only make the recipient feel cared for, but it can also make you feel lighter and happier.

8.2 Kindness Self-Care to treat yourself

Another great approach to cultivate self-sympathy is to take the empathy you feel for the people you love and redirect it towards yourself.

To do this, think of an aspect of your personality that you dislike and constantly criticize yourself for.

It can be something that has caused you to feel humiliated, embarrassed, guilty, or just generally bad about yourself. Now imagine that someone you love—your best friend, a family member or your significant other—is in the same circumstance. Imagine they come to you because they feel bad about that aspect of their personality and want some comfort.

How would you react? What would you say to them? Odds are you will try to be as understanding, caring, and supportive as possible, rather than condemning and judging them.

Now ask yourself the following question. Why shouldn't you be as understanding, caring, and supportive of yourself?

If your response is to be compassionate, this may help you question your self-analysis and consider being progressively more humane toward yourself.

The more you work on taking a self-compassionate viewpoint, the more natural it will become, eventually driving you to value your thoughts, emotions, and behaviors and react in an increasingly self-caring way.

8.3 Why you have to introduce Self-Care into Your Life

When people hear the term "self-care," the first image that's likely to pop into their mind is of a warm bath, a glass of wine, and maybe some chocolates—or something along those lines. While this kind of indulgence may very well be a self-caring activity, that's not all there is to it.

Self-care is any action that improves your mental and physical health, especially in stressful times. It also means eliminating unhealthy or toxic practices, mindsets, and behavior patterns.

Think about how young children need the care and support of a loving parent in order to feel safe and valued. They also need that parent to establish boundaries so they don't get hurt. Self-care is essentially becoming that kind of loving parent for yourself.

Practicing self-care won't eliminate stressful or painful experiences from your life, but it will help you manage and endure them better. You'll be less inclined to intensify your agony by putting up a fight against your own feelings. Instead, you will allow yourself to feel the way you do, accept that that's just the way things are, and begin the process of getting better.

As we have mentioned many times before, a self-compassionate and self-caring attitude toward yourself will not only help you feel more solid and comfortable with yourself, it will also vastly improve your relationships with other people.

Instead of engaging in a chain reaction of negative thoughts and feelings during a conflict with your partner, you will be able to remain grounded in the present moment.

This will, in turn, allow you to adopt a more objective perspective on your problems and solve them more efficiently.

If you're wondering whether self-care is really beneficial instead of only a passing trend, you might be surprised to know that there is scientific research backing up its usefulness.

One such study, "What are the Benefits of Mindfulness" (Davis and Hayes, 2012), was published in the American Psychological Association magazine.

It demonstrated that self-care can drastically diminish negative thoughts and stress, increase the ability to self-regulate and stifle interruptions, reduce explosive reactions, improve intellectual adaptability, enhance self-understanding, increase empathy, and reduce mental pain. While this might seem like esoteric mumbo jumbo, more and more scientists are beginning to get on board the mindfulness train.

There is a catch, though. Self-care isn't as easy as taking a pill. It takes practice—lots of it. Don't worry, you can start slow and gradually build up to some outstanding self-care techniques. Start by simply being in the present moment, really and truly.

A common practice for this is the 5-4-3-2-1 technique. Name five things you can see around you, four things you can touch, three things you can hear, two things you can smell, and one thing you can taste.

Another excellent practice is, of course, meditation. Don't close the book! Hear us out. You don't have to be a Zen master of meditation to enjoy the benefits of this practice. There are dozens of apps and hundreds of YouTube videos with fully-guided meditations that range from five to fifteen minutes. Doing this even just once a day can have remarkable effects on your mental health.

Many people think they can't meditate or that they'll do it "wrong" because they'll get distracted. Here's a secret, though.

There is no wrong way to meditate. You can be sitting down, lying down, or standing up. You can be in your bedroom, your car, a beautiful park, or your bathroom. It doesn't matter.

The only requirement is to be with yourself in the present moment. You don't have to clear your mind of all thoughts, either. If you find that you're getting intrusive thoughts while trying to meditate, simply acknowledge the thought, try to observe it from an objective and detached point of view, and let it go when you're ready. An excellent way to do this is to focus on your breath.

Don't worry too much about interruptions. If you live with other people, you can ask them not to disturb you for the next few minutes. If there's too much noise, try not to get discouraged. Think that the noise is just a part of life, a part of your present moment.

Acknowledge it, but don't let it bother you.

Now we're going to offer our own version of a simple meditation practice that you can start with. Feel free to following along even as you're reading and incorporate it into your daily life.

1. Get into a comfortable position. As mentioned before, you can be sitting or lying down for this. The only requirement is that you're comfortable. Take a few minutes to make sure your legs, back, and neck are not in any pain.

2. Move your attention to your breath. Inhale and feel the air enter your body through your nose. Give the air a pleasing, calming color in your mind's eye. Imagine this cool, colored breeze traveling all the way to your lungs. Imagine it gathering all the stress, bad thoughts, and negative experiences—the air will likely change colors at this point. Then exhale, letting your breath take all that negative energy out of your body.

3. Notice the sensations in your body. Feelings always, always, manifest in the body in one way or another.

As such, it can be exceptionally advantageous to associate your own feelings with sensations in your body. To start with, bring your attention to the soles of your feet. You can even tense them for a couple of seconds and then relax them again. Repeat this with every part of your body, gradually moving up from your feet to your legs, your torso, your arms, your hands, your neck, and finally, your face and head. Make a note of how everything feels. Do you feel your muscles relaxing? Is your heart rate slowing down?

If you feel pain or discomfort anywhere, direct the healing breath to that point and exhale the aches out. Feel free to make small, gentle adjustments to the positioning of your body.

4. Don't fight your thoughts. Your mind will eventually try to wander away from your breath and the present moment. This is a fact. Don't let it stress you out, though. The Buddhist portrayal of our thoughts as a "monkey mind" explains it well.

Your brain is always eager and wild, bouncing frantically, jumping from one thought to the next. When this happens, make a note of it.

Consider the thought, give it the attention it wants, and then let it float away. You have to make the conscious decision to bring your focus back to your breath.

Having a prepared statement such as, "I don't have to think about this right now.

I'm going to move my attention back to my breath." Do so gently, with self-compassion.

5. Don't sweat outside interruptions. When you become aware of diversions outside of yourself—barking dogs, car alarms, heavy trucks going by—make a note of it. You can handle it in a similar way to how you deal with your thoughts. "A dog is barking next door. But that doesn't need to bother me.

I'm going to move my attention back to my breath."

6. Slowly come out of it. Once you've finished scanning, tensing, and relaxing each body part, take a few more deep breaths.

You can remain in this state of profound relaxation for as long as you want. When you're ready to come out of it, bring your awareness back to your body, the ground beneath you, and the sounds around you.

Whenever you're ready, open your eyes. As mentioned before, meditation practice doesn't have to go on for hours on end. Doing it once a day for five minutes is enough. If you ever feel like you can do it for longer, go for it, but don't feel pressured to do so.

Here's another secret about meditation. You don't actually have to be sitting down with your eyes closed to do it. You can do it while driving, cooking, showering, walking from place to place, or even working out.

All you need to do is bring yourself to the present moment by concentrating on your breath, sensations in your body, and tangible things around you.

For example, as you walk from your car to your workplace, focus on the feel of your leg muscles as you lift and lower them. Take notice of the impact of your foot on the ground and feel how the heaviness of your body shifts from one foot to the other.

As you practice mindfulness, you may begin to notice and identify specific feelings as negative or undesirable. If you can, make a note of these feelings and explore them later on using your thoughts and feelings diary. Once you've done this, bring your attention back to your breath. If the feeling is too intense, don't be discouraged.

Stop the meditation and come back to it when you feel more settled. Or, if you feel like you can handle the feeling, try staying with it until you no longer feel troubled by them, or you believe you have done this enough.

The objective isn't to eliminate the feeling completely, but to face them with self-compassion, patience, and tolerance. You can go back and re-read Chapter 6 either before doing this activity or simultaneously with it.

8.4 Stay Strong

Another form of self-care is taking care of your physical health. Many people let this aspect of their lives fall by the wayside in stressful times. It's very common for people to forego eating healthy meals, sleeping the right amount of time, exercising, taking their medications, and sometimes even personal hygiene when they're going through a particularly rough time.

Taking care of yourself may sometimes seem like an impossible task. To make it easier on yourself, keep reminders around the house or on your phone to do the following small but vital things:

Drink water

Eat as healthy as you can

Get enough sleep (no, sleep isn't for the weak. It's indispensable if you want to stay healthy)

Exercise (even if it's just a ten-minute walk around the block) Take a shower

Making these essential activities into a habit will drastically improve your health. You'll feel more energetic and open to the happy moments in your life.

8.5 Feed Your Spirit

Research has also shown that belief in a higher power—whether you call it God, Buddha, Allah, nature, the universe, science—can lead to a more fulfilled life.

This involves looking at your qualities, good and bad, considering what is truly important in your life, and discovering a sense of wonder for your surroundings.

Many people refer to this as a quest for the holy or finding their faith. While religion and spirituality can certainly help some people accomplish this goal, those are not the only paths people can take to encounter this sense of wonder and love of life.

Regardless of your higher power of choice, such a quest can help you in your journey to self-awareness and vulnerability. It can also help you to adapt more easily to adverse events, recognize when a situation is out of your control, and be able to let go of it.

Depending on your inclinations, this can be accomplished by praying, meditating, attending religious services, volunteering for a cause you care about, communing with nature, and spreading love to other people. And yes, even going to therapy and taking your prescribed medications—science can also be regarded as a power bigger than an individual.

Life can be hard. Extremely hard. Sometimes all we really need is some sympathy and solace. However, the vast majority of us attempt to comfort ourselves with the most readily available practices, such as overeating, drinking excessively, shopping, gambling, etc.

Make a list of approaches you can take to meet your spiritual needs. You can do this by doing some research first and then adapting the ideas you like into something that works for you.

If you feel stuck in risky or unhealthy coping mechanisms, you can alternatively turn to an expert for assistance, such as a therapist, a priest, or whoever you feel comfortable with.

8.6 The importance of gratitude

You've probably heard this one before, and there's a good reason for

it. Research has consistently demonstrated that people who practice

gratitude are generally happier and more at peace than people who

don't.

There are many great gratitude exercises out there, so we're going to name a few.

Keep a gratitude journal. This is pretty self-explanatory. Write down a list of things you're grateful for each day. It's usually recommended that you do this before bed, but you can do it whenever you have some spare time. Try to list at least five things, and try doing this at least once a day, every day. It might be difficult to come up with things you're grateful for at first, but remember that everything counts, even if it's small and seems meaningless. You can use your thoughts and feelings diary or use a different one specifically for this activity.

Keep a gratitude jar. This is a slight variation of the previous exercise. Using Post-It notes or small slips of paper, write as many things that you're grateful for as you can think of. Fold the slips of paper and put them all in a jar. Every day, or whenever you're having a difficult time, pull a slip of paper from the jar and read it. You can add more bits of paper if you come up with more things you're grateful for.

Recognize how far you've come. Try thinking about your past self. This could be the "you" from ten years ago, two years ago, or just last week. Write down a list of personality traits or behavior patterns that your past self had and that you now consider to be negative or unhealthy. Simply recognizing these attitudes as harmful and acknowledging them is a big step. If you want to take it one step further, though, write down the ways you're actively trying to stop these toxic behaviors and how successful you've been so far. You will gradually start to see how far you've come on your mindfulness journey, proving how self-aware, compassionate, kind, and determined you are.

8.7 make new friends

A great way to make new friends throughout your journey to self-awareness is to put yourself in a position to meet people you share interests with.

Think about the things that make you happy. What do you genuinely enjoy doing? Look for clubs, associations, or classes you can join. It's especially useful to look for activities that give you the chance to meet new people.

Show interest and curiosity in the people around you and try striking up a conversation. You might find that you have a lot in common with one or two people and soon a friendship will develop.

The ideal way to build lasting friendships is to focus on one to three people at a time. This ensures that your energy and attention aren't stretched out too thin, as well as enabling you to truly get to know the other person.

If you feel a genuine connection with someone, share more about yourself, including your thoughts, feelings, and past experiences.

Remember what you learned in Chapter 7? Now's the time to put it into practice. Actively listen to what your new friend says. Use paraphrasing, verification, and validation techniques to make sure you really understand their point of view.

Chapter 9: Light Up Your Love Life

The concept of looking for a romantic partner is fundamentally simple: look for a like-minded person to share your life with. Putting this into practice is more complicated, though.

When you enter into a romantic relationship, you'll also start to understand the meaning of love and how it affects your daily life.

You will discover your weaknesses and how you interact with the people around you.

For many people, finding the right romantic partner is very challenging. We meet a lot of people throughout our lives and may even start romantic relationships. But those relationships soon end, in many cases, due to a lack of compatibility.

When you apply mindfulness to the search for your ideal significant other, the chances of finding the right match increase exponentially. Finding a person who loves you for who you really are doesn't have to be an impossible task. With self-awareness and self-compassion, you will undoubtedly find your ideal partner.

9.1 Relationship Goals

The very first thing you should do before looking for a romantic partner is to ask yourself what you really want and need from a relationship. Wanting a romantic partner to stop being lonely is a valid thought, but it's not a strong enough foundation for any kind of relationship.

Before meeting someone new, you should try looking objectively at what type of person would be right for you.

We've already mentioned that your childhood experiences will dictate your attachment style, as well as your ideal match based on your behavior patterns and core beliefs. However, regardless of specifics, there are three fundamental attributes in a romantic relationship you should consider.

Emotional availability: Just as young children need their parents or guardians to be emotionally open for them to feel safe, adults also require an emotional connection in order to thrive. Whenever something causes a distance between you and your partner, and this gap goes unaddressed, the relationship might start to fail. The further apart we grow from our significant other, the more alone, neglected, and abandoned we feel. This can ultimately serve as a basis for the relationship to end.

A port in a storm: Much like children running to their mom when distressed, adults in a stable relationship turn to one another when they need consolation or support during trying times. Having a trustworthy companion who can offer solace, help, and reprieve from life's inevitable hardships can be a real blessing.

People who have this "port in a storm" can potentially be less overwhelmed by life's difficulties. Therefore, if your partner is emotionally unavailable and distant, you will likely choose not to turn to them when you feel stressed.

Or, if you do look to them for comfort, they might be incapable of offering it.

A safe haven: To feel satisfied and fulfilled in your everyday life, it's essential for you to have the option to go after your deepest desires—or even just to have the opportunity to investigate what those desires might be. Stable and healthy relationships are the ones in which both people support and encourage each other to pursue their dreams.

As you consider these characteristics of a stable relationship, note that the two people involved must each make an effort and meet each other halfway for it to work out. Both people should also learn to be tolerant of each other. This will guarantee a place of refuge, empowerment, and support in tough situations, thus making the relationship a safe haven from which to interact with the world.

Although an individual's main concern might be finding a partner that can offer them all the attributes described above, you must be equipped to provide the same thing in return. Therefore, you must be prepared to give and receive these things.

While the above descriptions give you an idea of what you should strive for, they lack the subtleties of picking a partner who is right for you and how to continue from that point. We'll go into these details now.

9.2 The perfect Romantic Partner

A popular opinion of the ideal companion is someone who inspires you to be the best version of yourself. As you look for a romantic partner, consider people who display the following attributes.

Good communication skills: People who are good at expressing themselves, as well as listening to others, are much more likely to understand and support you and maintain healthy relationships. They can likewise effectively work through conflicts and differences. Generally speaking, good listeners and communicators are more adept at identifying and dealing with their feelings. This has the potential to translate well into a genuine emotional connection.

Compatibility: This should probably go without saying, but there must be some form of mutual interest between two people for the relationship to work out. This doesn't mean that you have to like the same things, or else your relationship is doomed.

However, engaging in activities together, making time to discuss and set goals for your relationship, and trying to be on the same page when solving conflicts is critical for a relationship to work.

Appreciation for who you are: Romance and passion are all well and good, but they're far from sufficient if you want a long-lasting relationship.

It's crucial that your partner expresses appreciation for who you are. You should both endeavor to get to know each other better, to truly understand each other, and to accept both flaws and qualities.

Emotional availability and willingness to grow: People who are mostly content with themselves or willing to grow and evolve are more likely to be emotionally available for their partners. They also have the ability to perceive themselves and their actions objectively, which allows them to recognize their shortcomings and admit to their mistakes. Because they know that every living person has flaws, they are also more open to understand and forgive their partner's missteps.

Being ready for a relationship: Your potential partner must be willing and prepared to focus on the relationship.

This means giving the relationship the required amount of time and energy, both when you're together and apart. They must be ready to commit to you and all the responsibilities that come from being in a relationship.

9.3 Perfect Relationship

Let's play a little game. Imagine that you're walking along a deserted beach. You're busy practicing mindfulness and self-awareness—maybe even meditating?—when you notice something shiny protruding from the sand. It's an old wedding band. You pick it up, dust off the sand, and suddenly a genie comes flying out! And wouldn't you know it, the genie tells you she has the power to invoke your ideal romantic partner! You name it, you got it. All she needs is a list of all the things you want in a companion. Of course, you know that you need to think very carefully before replying—the success of your future relationship depends on it.

You decide to make a detailed rundown of your ideal partner to help you with this undertaking. You need to incorporate all the characteristics you can possibly think of: personality, how they deal with conflict, how they relate to other people, how they relate to you, whether or not they want children, whether or not they want pets, occupation, physical attributes, way of life, needs, and interests. The more details you provide, the better.

Obviously, there is no genie (sorry!), and you will likely never meet

anyone person who fits everything on your list. However, by doing this activity, you will become more aware of what you truly want and need from a relationship.

This will increase the probability that you will choose to be with someone who is a solid match for you.

The right romantic partner is the one that supports you as you grow more self-confident and works alongside you to improve yourrelationship. However, that goes both ways. As such, consider what resources you have that maintain a stable relationship, and how you can change and evolve to be better at supporting your partner. As you do so, remember that building such a relationship will require a significant investment—this is because creating closeness requires some serious energy, and you won't be instantly relieved of your insecurities at any point in the process. Consider the following questions as you envision your ideal relationship.

• How will it influence you to have a mindful and stable partner?

• How do you imagine this relationship will feel like, in contrast to your past relationships?

• What are the characteristics that make that relationship superior to your past relationships?

• As your relationship-related stress decreases with your ideal partner, what would you do to bring light into your relationship? What unique methods would you use in this ideal relationship that are different from what you did in your past ones?

• In what better ways will your ideal partner help your deal with your relationship-related anxiety?

• How will this relationship help you to maintain your recently discovered self-confidence?

Write your answers down so you can go over them as many times as you want. Use them to envision your ideal relationship.

Allow it to truly sink in. Becoming acquainted with your deepest desires will help you obtain the knowledge of what you are actually looking for.

When coming up with the qualities you want from your partner, you might think to yourself that you'll "just know" when you meet the right person for you. We've been conditioned to believe that we'll receive some sign from above or within when we encounter our soulmate.

But this isn't something we can count on happening in real life. Often, we become infatuated with someone because of their looks or the personality traits that they keep close to the surface.

Attachment styles should also be taken into consideration. While you

don't have to have the exact same attachment style as your partner, both of you have to be willing to accept each other's peculiarities.

Regardless of whether your partner's requirements for emotional closeness matches yours, consider whether you actually feel supported by them when you express your needs, or whether you are sacrificing those parts of yourself for the sake of your relationship.

You may likewise discover that your insecurities make it hard to accept it if your partner wants to break up. This happens when people lose themselves in the relationship and give more of themselves to their partner than they can afford.

However, with mindfulness as your guide, you will be able to find a way through the hardship of a breakup. You can accomplish this by being empathetically in tune with your thoughts and feelings and thinking critically and objectively about the reason behind the breakup (mentalization). So always try to remember the experiences about yourself that you've picked up so far in this book.

If you belong to the avoidant attachment side of the spectrum, you

should keep in mind that your natural detachment might confuse or even hurt your partner. Particularly if they're on the anxious side of things.

You might even end up in a relationship with someone as independent and emotionally withdrawn as you are. This might seem ideal, but be careful not to neglect your genuine thoughts and feelings. The fact that both you and your partner are emotionally distant could end up making you feel even lonelier.

Without practicing mindfulness, people will regularly feel the need to impose their core beliefs on their relationship, rather than finding a middle ground with their partner. If you come to realize that your partner isn't willing to meet you halfway, you might decide that ending the relationship is the best course of action.

This requires that you take an objective—and even cold—look at the relationship.

Examine the ways in which your partner is unwilling or incapable of helping you build a stable, mindful, healthy relationship. Next, take another look at your answers at the beginning of this chapter concerning your ideal relationship.

This will help you realize that your current situation isn't worth your time and energy and that it's time to move on.

Breakups can be extremely painful, whether you practice mindfulness or not. Sometimes people can't handle the separation and end up getting back together. Be careful of this reaction, though.

It's up to you to decide whether or not you think your partner can change enough for your relationship to work.

The sad reality is that, more often than not, after enough time has passed, you'll both be right back where you started and will most likely break up again.

Or remain together but unhappy.

Although being separated can be agonizing, remembering the very real and valid reasons you broke up (namely, that your partner wasn't giving you what you needed) can help get past the pain.

Going back to such a person won't make you happy, though.

In the long run, it will be healthier for you to move on, heal from your breakup, and find someone who can give you what you need. We'll talk more about this in Chapter 11, where you'll learn to acknowledge and accept the need to end a relationship, as well as the best methods to do so

9.4 How to Find Support

Imagine a spiderweb. Note that it is held up by numerous strings. Even if you cut one, the web won't fall from its place. Like the little spider living in its web, you are supported by numerous "strings." These could be your family, friends, significant other, therapist, hobbies, etc. If you just depend on one person to feel loved and supported, you will want to hold on to that person for dear life. This urgent need to keep that person by your side will blind you to the unhealthy aspects of your relationship.

Create bonds with your family members, friends, coworkers, or anyone you feel comfortable with. Make sure your romantic partner is giving you what you need. Make it so that your life is held up by all the strings you could possibly want in order to flourish as a person.

Some people choose to shield themselves from getting too focused or absorbed in a romantic relationship in its early stages. Some even date multiple people at once. Knowing that there are numerous potential partners out there, you will feel genuinely more liberated to take as much time as you need in settling on one individual.

If you are open to casual dating, you have the advantage of choosing whether a specific relationship is promising. If this sounds like something you feel comfortable doing, amazing!

Take the plunge!

The sign of a strong relationship is feeling supported and encouraged by your partner. You will see them as a source of comfort and love. You'll both work hard to maintain the relationship, cultivating a sense of safety and intimacy.

Chapter 10: Keep Your Relationship alive

The best part of enjoying such a supportive bond is that you feel secure in yourself and your relationship.

According to research, a healthy and successful relationship is based on a sense of security.

The more confident you feel, the stronger your relationship will become. You can feel even more assured when you find a partner who is emotionally available and provides a supportive role in your life.

In such a relationship, both of you will appreciate each other, share your thoughts and feelings, communicate successfully, and trust one another.

You both have to be true to yourselves to be able to trust each other. Even in worst-case scenarios, you will both try to coordinate with each other to maintain a successful relationship.

You'll discover the best approaches to understanding and working on the differences between you and your partner. Remember to avoid trying to change your partner according to your requirements.

Try using mentalization to understand them instead.

10.1 Discover Yourself Relying on Each Other

You will gradually discover many things about your new relationship, the more you get to know your partner.

The level of understanding and compatibility with your significant other will serve as an indicator of how strong your relationship is. For example, if one of you shares something persona and the other reacts with compassion, understanding, and also discloses something personal.

Sharing personal information can help create a strong bond of affection and trust in a relationship.

As you spend more and more time together, you likewise build up a feeling of compassion and trust in one another's company.

Being in a relationship based on give-and-take or mutual sharing

might become troublesome if you have an insecure attachment style.

Your anxious need for closeness could cause you to feel powerless if you share your secrets. As a result, you may remain distant and become unavailable most of the time. In both scenarios, you are risking your relationship with your partner.

Primarily, your main focus is to understand how your partner will help you or hurt you.

This particular thing will keep on interfering between you and your partner and can also cause misunderstandings, which are solely based on misperceptions.

In case your way of disclosing your thoughts and feelings to your partner has caused damage to your relationship in the past, then it might be time to go about it in a different way. Start by thinking about your motivations for opening up to or withholding information from your partner.

Self-awareness is crucial for this. Start thinking critically about how and when you disclose certain information. This will help you in analyzing the situation more accurately.

If you're pushing yourself closer to your partner only to get away from your loneliness, then think again and evaluate your actions. Try to spend time with your old or new friends. To occupy yourself, you can also find an activity that can keep you busy and make you feel happy, safe, and validated. You can also devote your energy and time to a charity or volunteer work.

Instead of looking only toward your partner for comfort, try to find new ways to overcome your problems. Remember that there are many strings holding you up—don't neglect them. In this way, you can build a sense of connection, both with your partner and with other people in your life, all the while establishing a sense of trust and harmony.

It's simply not possible to develop a relationship in which you and your partner don't rely on each other to a certain extent. This is one of the cornerstones of any healthy relationship. You should feel free to depend on one another for love and comfort, as both of you navigate through your lives.

To be able to rely on your partner and let them depend on you, you should measure their requirements for autonomy and closeness, as well as your own. When both of you feel that these requirements are not being met—and this will inevitably happen at some point in your relationship—you should try to fix issues together before making any rash decisions. Allowing yourselves to be vulnerable and communicating in such situations will make it easier for you to truly understand each other. This sense of understanding will help you to resolve the issues in your relationship more effectively.

Keeping an open mind to your and your partner's viewpoints will also contribute to eliminating any negative thoughts. Whenever a problem arises in a relationship, it's not uncommon for people to start thinking bad things about their partners. If this goes on unaddressed, it can drive a potentially fatal wedge into your relationship.

As we've mentioned before, never put all the blame on yourself when things go wrong in the relationship. Remember to practice self-

compassion, first and foremost. Resolve your issues alongside your partner rather than carrying the weight of them alone. The two of you are a team, and you both need each other's love, compassion, comfort, and reassurance to build intimacy.

10.2 Boost your Intimacy

Speaking of intimacy, there are many different ways to cultivate it in your relationship. Dancing or exercising together is a great way to grow closer to your partner. Essentially, any activity that you both enjoy doing will guide you in the right direction of maintaining a healthy relationship.

Once you overcome the initial shyness in your relationship, you can become more open and vulnerable with your partner, which will also increase intimacy.

Remember that there no specific formula for a balanced amount of independence and closeness between two people.

Different people tend to have different needs and desires, and these requirements are constantly changing. Your relationship will be successful when you both acknowledge, adapt, and accept each other's needs.

Flexibility between two people also brings positivity and closeness in relationships.

10.3 You have to find Your Anxious Attachment

In the event when you're strongly compelled to always be with your partner or feel that you're overly attached to them, assume the role of devil's advocate for a moment. Imagine doing all the things you enjoy doing, but imagine it without your partner. This can be anything that brings joy and happiness in your life. For example, taking a class, starting a garden, or spending the weekends with your friends. Just imagine how enjoyable and freeing it might be to do these things, even if your significant other isn't with you.

If this exercise causes you too much anxiety, you don't have to think about it right now. You're in no way obligated to do anything you don't want to do.

To overcome this anxiety, you can try communicating your feelings to the people who love and support you.

Think about having a iscussion with your partner as well when you feel ready to do so.

Focus on how your partner reacts after discovering that you have unresolved issues and need support. If you realize that they're supportive, don't hesitate to share your thoughts and feelings about your situation.

If you find that your partner is reluctant to understand you or unsupportive, urge them to tell you why they feel that way.

It could be that his justifications are perfectly reasonable. Maybe your partner was never taught to help someone else with their problems, or they feel inadequate. If that's the case, have a calm discussion about both your issues. With enough patience, self-awareness, and empathy, you will soon find a solution to your problems.

10.4 Connection

After the honeymoon phase has passed, your relationship will start being affected by you and your partner's personal and professional hardships. Because of this, it can feel like you're losing the sense of closeness with your partner. People living with attachment-related anxiety can be particularly affected by this.

You have to keep in mind that this is a normal step for any

relationship. But just because your relationship is settling down and

your lives are returning to normal, it doesn't mean that your bond will

break. On the contrary, this is when true closeness and intimacy begin to appear.

Even so, you and your partner should take appropriate measures to avoid the issue of distance. With the help of all the mindfulness exercises that you now know, you should engage in discussions about this issue.

If you feel that you and your partner are becoming more and more distanced, these few basic steps can help make you feel close once more.

10.5 Keep yourself engaged with your soulmate

Interacting daily with your partner can help you in overcoming the communication gap. Make a routine of talking with your partner every day. Ask them about their day, what made them happy, and their plans for the next day. This conversation will help you both in staying synchronized and give a chance to support one another through both exciting and difficult times. It doesn't matter if you talk for an hour or ten minutes. Talking regularly and getting an update from your partner is what's important.

This conversation will be more fruitful if you and your partner have similar interests and hobbies. This way, you can pursue your own interests by following your partner's interests. This activity will bring a positive impact on your relationship.

10.6 Share experiences

Sharing your victories and struggles with your partner is one of the main things that will bring you closer together. If two people in a relationship don't share their life experiences, the distance between them will only increase.

Sharing will also help you in identifying your compatibilities. So, try to make plans each week to spend quality time together to understand each other better. Go on walks, to the movies, for dinner, or just spend some alone time together.

Other activities you can do together include hiking, bicycling, swimming, going on a picnic, playing tennis, dancing, and traveling to new places.

10.7 Why you have to Work on a project with your partner

This is a fantastic way to increase harmony and love between you and your partner.

Starting a project together like redecorating your home, volunteering, taking a class, or learning a language is one of the healthiest and most fun activities that couples can engage in.

10.8 make visible actions for love

If you and your partner feel comfortable with visible displays of affection, try to make your partner feel special by kissing, hugging, or giving them gifts and compliments. These small actions of love can help you in growing closer to your partner.

10.9 Express always your feelings of love and happiness

Your partner should always know how important they are to you. This is something that often falls by the wayside when you've been with someone for a long time. But everyone needs to hear how much they matter to their significant other once in a while.

You can express your feelings through actions or words. Whichever option you choose depends on the situation.

The key is always to make an effort to express your love to your partner and make them feel special.

10.10 Compliment your soulmate

Most people love compliments. Especially when they come from our significant other. In a relationship, compliments and small gifts play a vital role in bringing people closer together. Whenever you find the moment or occasion, try to compliment your partner. It will bring energy and love to your relationship.

10.11 Find new ways to show all your love

If you feel your relationship is in a rut, try expressing your love in fresh new ways. You can give your partner a gift you made yourself, make them a playlist of songs that mean something to both of you, or surprise them with a weekend away.

10.12 Know when to yield

Acts of kindness and love in a relationship can be a tremendous help

when solving your problems. There are times when your relationship will face hardships, and both you and your partner can become inflexible on an issue. Think critically about the situation. Sometimes, a conflict just isn't worth the amount of energy that you're both giving it, or the sadness it brings. This is the time to make yourself flexible and accommodating of the situation.

By doing this, you are not only saving the love between you and your partner but will also save your relationship.

Chapter 11: Why you have to resolve the differences between you and your partner

Ups and downs are part of every relationship. Where there is love, there are conflicts, disagreement, and miscommunication as well. To minimize such events, many people try to avoid conflicts and do everything they can to maintain their partner's love and attention.

But by doing so, they tend to end up smothering their own feelings and needs.

Eventually, such people might realize that they're the only ones in their relationship who are making all the efforts to make the relationship work.

When you feel alone and taken for granted, you will experience hurt and maybe even depression, which could translate to feeling angry with your partner. This pattern will only lead to more adverse circumstances and will not make you happy.

There is a much better way you can adopt, though. With the help of compassionate self-awareness, you will be more tolerant of your emotions and learn to value yourself. You will become a more positive person and will be able to take positive feedback from the caring and loving people in your life.

Consequently, you will be able to ignore the negative energy and focus on your relationship's positive aspects. This will help to maintain an intimate relationship with your partner.

When you express yourself in healthy and mindful ways, your relationship will flourish. In this chapter, we will teach you some coping mechanisms to deal with the conflicts you face in the relationship.

11.1 Support

Asking your partner for support is the best approach to maintaining a nurturing relationship. Asking for what you want and need in a relationship helps to make the bond stronger.

There are two essential practices that help with this.

First, always share your wants, needs, and feelings with your partner.

If there's something you don't like about your partner's behavior, it's always better to tell them rather than bottling up your feelings.

Second, ask your partner concretely and directly what they want and need from you.

It is vital for both of you to know what the other is going through. This will make it easier for you to understand each other better.

When you try to solve your problems together, you will be on the same page, and resolving your issues will be easier.

If you want to discuss a particular issue with your partner, the best thing to do is to pick a neutral time and place for it. This means you should find a place where you both feel comfortable and safe and a time when you're both calm and relaxed. A difficult conversation has a higher chance of success if you're both ready to deal with it.

Tell your partner your problem as shortly and succinctly as possible. Get on the point, and explain how it affects you. Cut out any unnecessary details, especially accusations or assumptions of guilt. Avoid the blame game. Pinning the blame on you or your partner will only make you both defensive and emotionally distant

Show Empathy

We've already talked about the importance of empathy to maintain healthy relationships. Empathy is especially critical when trying to solve problems with your partner.

Try to see the situation and understand it according to your significant other's perspective. Empathize with your partner. In order to do this, you will have to put aside your own perspective and core beliefs.

To minimize your conflicts, you and your partner need to put yourself in each other's shoes and talk about your feelings supportively and constructively. This approach promotes a sense of safety, even in times of high vulnerability and personal conflict.

Whenever you need to have a difficult discussion with your partner, you need to prepare yourself to open up to compassion and forgiveness. You can obtain the best results when you go into such a conversation with the firm and explicit intent to understand your significant other.

You should always strive to be a safe haven for your partner and ask your partner to be one for you. You both need to feel safe with each other in order for the relationship to work. This can only happen when you focus on one person's problems at a time.

When one of you is explaining the problem or expressing your feelings, the other should listen and understand as best as possible.

When your partner sees that you're trying your best to empathize, they will be less defensive and feel more comfortable telling you everything that's bugging them. Your job here is to listen without interrupting.

Try to stay on topic while discussing a difficult subject. It's easy to

jump from one topic to another, especially if you have several

unresolved issues. Doing this isn't conducive to problem-solving,

though.

Respect is a vital element of every relationship. Always be respectful of your partner when you're in the middle of a heated discussion. Losing your temper and blowing up at your partner will significantly damage your relationship.

11.3 Forgive

Feeling hurt by something your significant other said or did is excruciating and can very difficult for people who have attachment-

related anxiety to handle. They're more prone to thinking that they're flawed and unworthy of love. This leads to self-criticism and makes the relationship toxic.

Whenever you get hurt by something that happened in your relationship, try maintaining an objective perspective.

As always, avoid the blame game and have an open conversation with your significant other. Then let go of the past and learn to forgive. By adopting the habit of forgiveness, you will be able to overcome the anger haunting your heart and soul.

11.4 How to Know If Your Relationship Is Really Worth It

If you're confused about whether your relationship is healthy or not, it might be time to take a critical look at it. Is your partner emotionally available? Are they responsive to your needs and wants? Do you feel loved and cared for?

Support and care are two of the most important elements of a relationship. Is your partner supportive in difficult times? Are they there for you when you feel sad and upset? Does your partner encourage you to pursue your dreams?

Because this is a two-way street, you should also ask yourself if you're there for your partner. Don't worry too much about achieving a perfect balance. The important thing is that you're both comfortable with the balance that does exist in your relationship.

If you end up realizing that your relationship is unhealthy and decide to end it, you should formulate a plan that will help you do this. Here are some recommendations that will help you.

Rely on your support system. Breakups are painful, and you will eventually need someone to lean on and share your feelings with. Share your struggles with the people who love and let them be there for you if you decide to end your relationship.

Remember that it's okay to feel sad and cry. When you lose an

important person in your life, it is natural to feel unhappy and lonely.

Do not push your feeling under the rug—this is very detrimental to

your mental health. Mourn your relationship and give yourself time to

heal.

Keeping reminding yourself that you are a valuable person. Always remember your strength and power. This might seem impossible to do in times of misery and sadness, but consider and pay attention to what your friends and family love and appreciate about you.

They wouldn't be in your life if they didn't genuinely enjoy your company.

Choose healthy ways of coping with your stress and sadness. When you're going through rough times, it can be easy to adopt unhealthy

habits.

Make an effort to take care of yourself, even if it seems difficult at first. Keep yourself busy with your favorite activities.

Listen to relaxing music, watch your favorite movies or TV shows, take long baths. Try to eat healthy and fresh food, go on walks or exercise, and get enough sleep. Anything that makes you feel better and doesn't compromise your mental and physical health should be your top priority after a breakup.

Doing volunteer work can bring a sense of meaning to your life, which can be an excellent remedy when you feel depressed or lonely.

Volunteer at shelters or schools to create a feeling of comfort and peace. Gardening is also very helpful in such cases.

Helping others brings helps you feel valuable and connected to other people.

Be prepared for the urge to get back together. There's a chance that you will think about getting in touch with your ex at some point after the breakup. You will almost exclusively remember the good times and come up with ways of doing things differently and better the second time around.

Before getting in touch with your ex or picking up their calls, think about the difficult times you went through together.

Remind yourself of all the reasons why you broke up. Talk to your close friends and family members, and discuss the situation. If you conclude once more that ending the relationship was the right decision, just keep in mind that this urge to see them again will pass.

Forgive yourself if you do try to go back to your ex. The feelings of sadness and loneliness might become too much for you to deal with, and you'll end up trying to reconnect with them. This doesn't mean you're weak.

We all need to feel connected to other people.

Sometimes, it's easier to go back to old relationships than to start new ones. If this happens, first you have to forgive yourself. Then try to think critically about the situation. Whether you stay with your partner and try again or decide to put an end to it is up to you.

11.5 Ending Note

We hope this book has provided you with the guiding light you needed to reshape your relationship. By making minor changes in your behavior patterns, you can create a path towards a healthy and happy relationship.

Compassion, understanding, and empathy are the key to a successful relationship.

Consult with a Professional

The information provided in this book is not meant to replace the help that you can get from a professional. If you or your partner suffer from a mental illness, it is highly recommended that you attend therapy. If you find that this book's guidance is not enough or you need help applying its concepts, consider couples therapy.

Develop a secure base with your therapist so that you can share everything you think and feel. Your therapist will guide you and help you to eliminate your problematic behaviors and negative self-perceptions.

Finding a therapist with whom you can emotionally connect is the best way to ensure you'll have the kind of heartfelt

discussions that can only be done with someone you feel safe with.

Conclusion

Anxiety in Relationships is a guide for all couples who face issues in their relationship. Sharing your life with someone is not easy. Anxiety can overshadow your love and commitment to your significant other. We hope that the exercises provided in this book will help you find the best solutions to your problems.

Applying the concepts found in this book can also help you to understand your partner better, and you'll be able to face anxiety or detachment issues in your relationship.

We urge you to work on the self-awareness, self-deception, mindfulness, and self-compassion exercises herein and prepare your mind to deal with any issue in a profound manner.

www.ingramcontent.com/pod-product-compliance
Lightning Source LLC
Chambersburg PA
CBHW071615080526
44588CB00010B/1137